Digital Literacy Skills

for FE Teachers

SAGE was founded in 1965 by Sara Miller McCune to support
the dissemination of usable knowledge by publishing innovative
and high-quality research and teaching content. Today, we
publish more than 850 journals, including those of more than
300 learned societies, more than 800 new books per year, and
a growing range of library products including archives, data,
case studies, reports, and video. SAGE remains majority-owned
by our founder, and after Sara's lifetime will become owned by
a charitable trust that secures our continued independence.

Los Angeles | London | New Delhi | Singapore | Washington DC

Digital Literacy Skills

for FE Teachers

Jonathan White

Los Angeles | London | New Delhi
Singapore | Washington DC

Learning Matters
An imprint of SAGE Publications Ltd
1 Oliver's Yard
55 City Road
London EC1Y 1SP

SAGE Publications Inc.
2455 Teller Road
Thousand Oaks, California 91320

SAGE Publications India Pvt Ltd
B 1/I 1 Mohan Cooperative Industrial Area
Mathura Road
New Delhi 110 044

SAGE Publications Asia-Pacific Pte Ltd
3 Church Street
#10-04 Samsung Hub
Singapore 049483

Editor: Amy Thornton
Production controller: Chris Marke
Project management: Deer Park Productions,
Tavistock, Devon
Marketing manager: Lorna Patkai
Cover design: Wendy Scott
Typeset by: C&M Digitals (P) Ltd, Chennai, India
Printed and bound by CPI Group (UK) Ltd,
Croydon, CR0 4YY

Library of Congress Control Number: 2015943492

British Library Cataloguing in Publication Data

A catalogue record for this book is available from the
British Library

ISBN 978-1-4739-0458-3 (pbk)
ISBN 978-1-4739-0457-6

At SAGE we take sustainability seriously. Most of our products are printed in the UK using FSC papers and boards.
When we print overseas we ensure sustainable papers are used as measured by the Egmont grading system.
We undertake an annual audit to monitor our sustainability.

CONTENTS

AUTHOR STATEMENT

Jonathan White is an experienced teacher and librarian. For the last decade he has worked in various education sectors in the UK, supporting learning, teaching and development in digital and information literacies. Jonathan works in the Department for Learning Enhancement at the University of Derby, supporting students and staff of both further and higher education programmes.

Jonathan received his MA from Loughborough University with a thesis on the teaching of IT skills in public libraries and he framed his PGCE work around the teaching of information literacy in a further education college. He is a member of the Society for Education and Training Foundation (SET) and the Chartered Institute of Library and Information Professionals (CILIP). He writes a blog on the teaching of digital and information literacies at teachdigitalliteracy.com and is on Twitter – @jonwhite82.

ACKNOWLEDGEMENTS

I would like to thank the following people for their encouragement and support during the process of researching and writing this book:

Helen Fairlie, Freelance Editor.

Amy Thornton, Senior Commissioning Editor for Education, Learning Matters.

Dr Jane Secker, Copyright and Digital Literacy Advisor, London School of Economics and Political Science.

Peter Scales, Lecturer in Education, University of Derby.

Amy White, Lecturer in Science, Macclesfield College.

Jeanette Kirk, Teacher of Computing, The Becket School.

Colleagues at the University of Derby and past colleagues at Rotherham College of Arts and Technology for their knowledge of, and passion for, excellent learning and teaching.

In this chapter you will learn:

- What is meant by the word 'digital' and how it is used in this book.
- The significance of the word 'digital' and related terminology for UK education sectors.
- Whom this book is aimed at and how it links to the Sector Professional Standards.
- About the acronyms and key terminology used throughout this book.

What do we mean by 'digital'?

The meaning of the word 'digital' has evolved over the past two decades as the Web and other Internet-connected technologies have become part of everyday life. The word 'digital' was originally used to refer to the expression of electronic data as 1s and 0s in computing processes (Oxford English Dictionary, 2014). Predominantly in the 1990s, the word 'digital' came to be synonymous with media and entertainment as music, video and television became available in higher-quality digital forms which replaced the old analogue systems.

In the twenty-first century, the word 'digital' can be found everywhere, with much of what is computer, Web and Internet-based being referred to using the word. We use it to describe:

- Internet-connected hardware and software – 'digital technologies', 'digital devices', 'digital tools', 'digital services'.

- Information and media available online to download or stream – 'digital content', 'digital media', 'digital video', 'digital audio'.

- Online and virtual environments and the 'world' we have created online – 'the digital world' and 'digital environments'.

- The interconnected and technologically advanced period we are living in – 'the digital age' and 'digital society'.

- The identities and personas we have online – 'digital profiles', 'digital citizens', 'digital learners', 'digital teachers' and 'digital workers'.

- Access and equality issues regarding the Internet – 'the digital divide', 'the digitally excluded' and 'digital inclusion'.

- The skills, knowledge, understanding, experiences and capabilities we each have with digital technologies – 'digital literacy', 'digital skills', 'digital capabilities', 'digital natives' and 'digital immigrants'.

- The process of learning, teaching and researching with digital technologies – 'digital learning', 'digital teaching', 'digital scholarship'.

- The changes to society and the 'real world' (referred to as the physical world in this book), which have occurred with the advancement of the digital age – 'the digital revolution'.

The word 'digital' is used in all of these contexts throughout this book and many of them will be examined, discussed and challenged.

Our digital lives

We are surrounded by, and immersed in, digital technologies. From surfing the Web, using apps and services, to communicating through social networks and interacting with digital content, digital technology usage forms part of our everyday lives, learning and work. The digital world allows us to do everything; from watching, reading or listening; sharing, discussing and organising; through to editing and publishing, and increasingly we can do it all from one device. These interactions could increase our knowledge and understanding, develop our skills, capabilities and confidence, enable us to get a new job or open the door to more opportunities. However, if we do not understand our interactions in the digital world, they could lead us to inadvertently break the law, acquire incorrect or false information and cause problems for us in the physical world.

A range of devices are available to us through which we can access and contribute to the digital world, but traditionally the most commonly used device has been a personal computer (PC). During the last decade, however, a wide range of digitally connected mobile devices have become part of our everyday lives. This includes smartphones, tablets, computers, e-book readers and digital media players. Statistics show that we are purchasing more of these devices than desktop PCs and laptops (Arthur, 2014) and almost sixty per cent of us are choosing to access the Internet in this way (Ofcom, 2014).

Now, in the second decade of the twenty-first century, devices we do not generally think of as computers are able to access the Internet and upload and download data. A new generation of smart-watches, personal health and exercise monitors, home heating systems, smart televisions, set-top boxes, digital video recorders (DVRs), home surveillance systems and even light-bulbs are part of our digital world, in what is being labelled the 'Internet of things'. This means that as well as communicating with humans we now also communicate with our objects and they can communicate with each other. Unimaginable amounts of data and information about us flow through the Internet, recording everything from details of financial transactions through to how many minutes we spend playing online games. As this data flows, it is collected and stored in numerous places to be used by individuals, companies, governments and other organisations.

The multifaceted nature of our use of digital technologies raises a number of questions, not only about how we understand and control our use of the Internet (although that is an extremely important question we will explore), but also, how we understand our lives and our place in the physical world in relation to what we do online in the digital world. It also questions what we as teachers can do to facilitate this understanding and the learning of relevant digital skills.

Education and the digital world

Across sectors of education, the digital world is having a profound effect, with the very notions of learning and teaching being questioned and redefined. Many have sought to bring the digital world into the classroom with the intention of improving traditional learning and teaching, engaging learners and aiding acquisition of new skills. This has mainly been through the addition of information and learning technologies (ILTs) such as interactive whiteboards (IWB), virtual learning environments (VLEs) and a wide range of digital technologies. Others have sought to question the very notion of traditional learning and teaching in the digital age, and seek to turn the digital world into a classroom. The rise of massive open online courses (MOOCs) and the use of digital media and content as learning resources being key examples. Wider debates on learning and teaching methods, the application of sound pedagogy and the practice and role of the teacher have as a result become key areas of discussion.

In recent times, the focus of educational debate around digital technologies has moved to pay more attention to the needs of individuals and specific groups, in order to identify best practices and the levels of fluency required to carry out a range of digital tasks. Teachers are then able to identify, understand and teach the knowledge, skills and abilities required in order to become an engaged, critical thinking and creative citizen of the digital world. This is how the idea of becoming 'digitally literate' has developed.

This book aims to enable you to understand and develop your own digital literacy and to apply it to your practice. This begins in Chapter 2 with a thorough introduction to what digital literacy means in the context of the Further Education (FE) and Skills sector and provides a basic framework for personal and professional development which will be referred to throughout this book.

Who is the audience for this book?

This book is aimed at anyone working to teach, lecture, tutor, assess, coach, facilitate or support learners in the FE and Skills sector. The term 'teacher' is used throughout this book to refer to all in these groups. The content is also applicable to those in middle and senior management posts, who may wish to consider some of the approaches discussed when planning staff development.

This book can be used as a basis for professional development in digital skills for those currently practising as teachers or those undertaking initial teacher training (ITT) in the FE and Skills sector.

You may have different reasons for using this book, but whatever your starting point, you should find it useful and applicable. The book is not written with particular levels in mind, as these are relative, but you should approach each chapter with your own starting point in mind. You will then be able to develop at your own pace and based upon your own needs. Here are some of the possible starting points you may currently be at:

- You feel that your digital skills are low and/or you do not use digital technologies very often. You can use this book to gain new understanding and knowledge of digital technologies and frame this around your current practice. You should focus on developing your knowledge, understanding and confidence as you work through this book.

- You are comfortable with your digital skills and/or are a capable user of digital technologies, but are struggling to embed them within your practice. You can use this book to consolidate what you already know and understand, and put your skills into action to improve your professional practice and learning and teaching. You may need to map your current knowledge and skills in digital technologies against the elements of your professional role. This may help you to become more creative and innovative in your use of digital technologies.

- You consider yourself to be a 'power user' of digital technologies, very adept in digital environments and have embedded digital skills and technologies into your professional practice and learning and teaching. You can use this book to plan for the next stage in your development and to consider new ideas, theories and practices. You may want to pay particular attention to the theory mentioned throughout the book, which allows you to build upon your current knowledge and skills and allows for deeper thinking about your own and others' usage of digital technologies.

Links to the sector professional standards

The UK government bodies with responsibility for setting standards within and supporting the UK's FE and Skills sector are currently undergoing unprecedented changes. With this, the professional standards for FE and Skills teachers are also changing. In 2013, the Education and Training Foundation (ETF) was given the remit to take over the work previously carried out by Lifelong Learning UK (LLUK) and the Learning and Skills Improvement Service (LSIS), as well as the responsibility for setting a new set of sector-wide professional standards. In late 2014, the Institute for Learning (IfL), which was the FE and Skills sector professional body and awarding body for Qualified Teacher Learning and Skills (QTLS), ceased to exist and passed their remit to the ETF. In May 2015, the ETF created the Society for Education and Training (SET), as the professional body for the FE and Skills sector.

In 2014, the ETF published a new set of sector professional standard for the FE and Skills sector which replaced the sector professional standards set in 2007 by LLUK (Lifelong Learning UK, 2007). The new Professional Standards for Teachers and Trainers in Education and Training – England are available to download from the SET website (ETF, 2014; SET, 2015), which has taken over development of the Sector professional standards from 2015 onwards. The digital literacy framework presented in Chapter 2, and mentioned in each subsequent chapter, has been mapped against these new professional standards and you can find this document in Appendix 1.

Table 1.1 Acronyms and key terminology used in this book

Acronym/term	Meaning/definition
BCS	Originally stood for British Computer Society, but they are now called 'BCS: The Chartered Institute for IT'
BIS	Department for Business, Innovation and Skills
BTEC	Originally stood for 'Business and Technician Education Council'. It is now a suite of qualifications awarded by Edexcel
BYOD	Bring your own device
CC	Creative Commons licensing scheme
CLA	Copyright Licencing Agency
CILIP	Chartered Institute of Library and Information Professionals
CMS	Content management system
CPD	Continuous professional development
CSS	Cascading style sheet
CV	Curriculum vitae
DCMS	Department for Culture, Media and Sport
DCSF	Department for Children, Schools and Families (now defunct and replaced by the Department for Education)
DfE	Department for Education
DIUS	Department for Innovation, Universities and Skills (now defunct and replaced by the Department for Business, Innovation and Skills)
DL	Digital literacy
DOAJ	Directory of Open Access Journals
DRM	Digital rights management
e-book	Electronic book
e-journal	Electronic journal
e-mail	Electronic mail
ETF	Education and Training Foundation
ERA	Educational Recording Agency
FAQ	Frequently asked questions
FE	Further Education
FELTAG	Further Education Learning Technology Action Group
FOSS	Free open source software
GCSE	General Certificate of Secondary Education
HE	Higher Education
HTML	Hyper Text Mark-up Language
ICT	Information and communication technology
IfL	Institute for Learning (now defunct Sector professional body, has been replaced by the SET)
IL	Information literacy

(Continued)

Table 1.1 (Continued)

Acronym/term	Meaning/definition
ILT	Information and learning technology
IT	Information technology
ITT	Initial teacher training
IWB	Interactive whiteboard
Jisc	Originally an acronym standing for 'Joint Information Systems Committee', but they are now known just as Jisc
Jisc RSCs	Jisc Regional Support Centres
LLUK	Lifelong Learning UK (now defunct, operations are part of the Education and Training Foundation)
LSIS	Learning and Skills Improvement Service (now defunct, operations are part of the Education and Training Foundation)
MOOC	Massive open online course
NEET	Not in education, employment or training
NLA	Newspaper Licensing Agency
NMC	New Media Consortium
NSPCC	National Society for the Prevention of Cruelty to Children
NVQ	National Vocational Qualification
OA	Open Access
OAI	Open Access Initiative
OERs	Open education resources
Ofcom	Office of Communications. Regulator of the UK communications industries
Ofsted	Office for Standards in Education, Children's Services and Skills
Ofqual	Office of Qualifications and Examinations Regulations
OGL	Open Government Licensing
PC	Personal computer
QCF	Qualifications and Credit Framework
RSS	Really simple syndication
SEO	Search engine optimisation
SET	Society for Education and Training (replaced the IfL as the Sector professional body. Managed by the ETF)
SFA	Skills Funding Agency
URL	Uniform Resource Locator
VLE	Virtual learning environment
VOOC	Vocational open online course
WWW	World Wide Web

Summary

In this chapter you have learned:

- What is meant by the word 'digital' and how it is used in this book.

- The significance of the word 'digital' and related terminology for UK education sectors.

- Who the audience for this book is and how it links to the Sector Professional Standards.

- About the acronyms and key terminology used throughout this book.

References

Arthur, C (2014) 'PC market doldrums will continue to 2018, says IDC', *Guardian*, 13 June. Available at: http://www.theguardian.com/technology/2014/jun/13/pc-market-doldrums-will-continue-to-2018-says-idc.

ETF (2014) *Professional Standards for Teachers and Trainers in Education and Training – England*. Available at: http://www.et-foundation.co.uk/supporting/support-practitioners/professional-standards/.

LLUK (2007) *New Overarching Professional Standards for Teachers, Tutors and Trainers in the Lifelong Learning Sector*. Available at: http://et-foundation.co.uk/vision/docs/external-documents/68-new-overarching-professional-standards/file.html.

Ofcom (2014) *The Communications Market Report 2014*. Available at: http://stakeholders.ofcom.org.uk/binaries/research/cmr/cmr14/2014_UK_CMR.pdf.

Oxford English Dictionary (2014) Definition of the word 'digital'. Available at: http://www.oxforddictionaries.com/definition/english/digital.

SET (2015) *Professional Standards*. Available at: https://set.et-foundation.co.uk/professionalism/professional-standards/.

2   WHAT IS DIGITAL LITERACY?

> In this chapter you will learn:
>
> - How digital literacy is defined by key organisations and theorists.
> - What digital literacy means in the context of the FE and Skills sector.
> - How digital literacy relates to other literacies and critical thinking.
> - The differences between ICT skills and digital literacy skills.
> - What knowledge, skills and abilities a digitally literate teacher needs to have.
> - About the digitally literate teacher framework used throughout this book.

This chapter explores definitions of the term 'digital literacy' and the knowledge, skills and practices associated with it. By the end of this chapter you should have a basic understanding of what digital literacy means as a general concept in education and more specifically how it relates to your professional practice in the FE and Skills sector. This will enable you to frame your development as a digitally literate teacher.

Introducing the idea of digital literacy

Before considering definitions of digital literacy, we first need to consider the factors that are influencing the development of the term 'digital literacy' and are pivotal to understanding the need for it.

The following changes to our relationship with digital technologies have occurred in the last decade:

- **Ownership of mobile 'Internet ready' digital devices is now the norm**. In the UK, over sixty per cent of adults now own a smartphone and forty four per cent of households have one or more tablet PCs, according to the communications regulator, Ofcom (2014: 4). Almost sixty per cent of adults say that they access the Internet through their mobile phone, in addition to other devices. The majority of mobile phones made within the last five years are Internet enabled, even if they are not a fully-fledged smartphone. Many of the apps, services and digital tools we use work by sending and receiving data through the Internet, even if we are not consciously using it.

- **Our usage of the Internet has changed because of social networks and media**. Social networks and media are extremely popular, and many people now use these services and apps as their main method of communication and media consumption. Over 500 million tweets are now sent worldwide everyday (Holt, 2013) and over 24 million people are estimated to be actively posting to Facebook every day (Glenday, 2013). Many people also post photographs to services such as Instagram and Flickr, upload videos to services such as YouTube and influence opinion by blogging, reviewing, editing and curating on sites like Blogger, Trip Advisor, Wikipedia and Pinterest.

- **The world's information and multimedia content is seemingly freely available 'on demand'.** Information and media on almost every subject are accessible, viewable and/or downloadable from the Web. We use search engines, apps and other digital tools to quickly find what we are looking for and use the results to inform our choices/decision-making, aid our learning and answer our questions.

- **Digital technologies, that is Internet-connected hardware and software, have significance in almost every aspect of our lives.** We now use the Internet for leisure, for work, for organisation and for entertainment. Have we changed how we live our everyday lives because of the Internet, or has the Internet changed and adapted to fit how we live and work? Have we developed new skills and new communication methods because of the Internet, and how will we continue to evolve with the Internet?

As these changes take place in society, the FE and Skills sector is changing to embrace digital technologies, teach vital digital skills and lead educational developments in the digital age:

- **Delivering more FE and Skills sector learning online.** Stemming from the recommendations of the Further Education Learning Technology Action Group (FELTAG, 2013), the Skills Funding Agency (SFA, 2014) is recommending that ten per cent of the delivery of FE programmes moves to be self-directed online learning, rather than face to face. The sector is also embracing massive open online courses (MOOCs) and finding ways to reach more learners through digital technologies than ever before.

- **Creating a digitally skilled workforce in the UK.** By working with employers the FE and Skills sector is responding to their needs and embedding digital skills into programmes.

- **Enabling all learners to get online and use digital technologies.** The sector is well placed to ensuring equality of access to the Internet and digital skills, and is part of national initiatives to tackle digital exclusion.

- **Engaging learners with digital technologies and encouraging creativity and agility with digital tools.** Through innovating with classroom technologies, teachers are learning new digital skills and are enhancing the learning of their students with the use of a wide range of digital devices, software, apps and other tools.

- **Improving critical thinking around digital information and media, reducing plagiarism and tackling the 'cut and paste' culture.** Teachers across the sector have been acutely aware of these issues for several years, but with more learners progressing to higher education than ever before and more explicit requirements for referencing on marking schemes, the need to enhance learning and teaching around these topics is increasing.

Activity

Having read about the changes above, think about how you use digital technologies in both your personal and professional life:

- *Which of the above are going on at your institution (whether you are involved or not)?*

- *What specific knowledge and skills do you have in each?*

- *Can you identify good practice in both your personal and professional uses of digital technologies and transfer it between them?*

It is clear that we are each forming intricate and complex relationships with digital technologies in both a personal and professional capacity. For the teacher, this means that we have to understand and develop our knowledge, skills, confidence and capabilities with digital technologies in order to become competent, creative and critical with them personally and professionally, but also so that we can educate and support learners in doing so themselves.

Definitions of digital literacy

[Digital literacy is about] mastering ideas, not keystrokes

An early thought on digital literacy by Paul Gilster
in 1997 (in Bawden, 2008: 18)

Digital literacy = digital tool knowledge + critical thinking + social engagement

Definition presented on the *Guardian* website
by Josie Fraser (in Anyangwe, 2012)

The term 'digital literacy' has formed to encompass all aspects of developing the knowledge, skills, competencies, confidence and capabilities needed to use, interact with, communicate through, learn with, work with, and create with digital technologies. By becoming digitally literate we can learn to make use of digital technologies in a productive, creative, critical, safe, and ethical way.

Formal definitions of digital literacy with specific relevance to the FE and Skills sector have been formulated by Jisc and the British Computer Society (BCS). Jisc is a UK government-funded body which provides advice and guidance on ICT and digital resources to the FE and Skills and Higher Education (HE) sectors. They define digital literacy as:

> *Those capabilities which fit an individual for living, learning and working in a digital society... Digital literacy looks beyond functional IT skills to describe a richer set of digital behaviours, practices and identities. What it means to be digitally literate changes over time and across contexts, so digital literacies are essentially a set of academic and professional situated practices supported by diverse and changing technologies.*

(Jisc, 2014)

In 2013, the BCS launched their *Digital Literacy for Life Programme* with the aim of encouraging the development of digital skills, learning and teaching across the UK (BCS, 2013a). Their definition of digital literacy deals with similar issues to the one presented by Jisc:

> [Digital literacy is] those capabilities that mean an individual is fit for living, learning and working in a digital society. Digital literacy is about being able to make use of technologies to participate in and contribute to modern social, cultural, political and economic life.

(BCS, 2013b)

These definitions may seem wide in scope, but they are a succinct way of covering the breadth of scenarios in which we use digital technologies and the purposes we use them for. As the Jisc definition indicates, what it means to be digitally literate could be a fluid concept, with different situations requiring different knowledge and skills. The technological landscape is continually advancing and changing, so we must be prepared to continually review and update our digital practice. At the heart of digital literacy is the need to develop a critical, creative and productive approach to using digital technologies, which, once developed as a mindset, can be applied to whatever changes occur. As teachers, this mindset is already a key element of our professionalism. In Chapters 2 and 3 we shall begin to explore how our digital practice is shaped and developed, and Chapter 10 specifically looks at planning for further professional development around digital technologies and reflection on digital development.

Both definitions also highlight the need to understand our own goals and our place in society, as we use digital technologies. This is an increasingly important part of all digital technologies users' development as creative, informed and responsible citizens. The Jisc Regional Support Centres' (Jisc RCSs) *Digital Literacies Organisational Review* document elaborates further on this:

> If learners are to participate socially, culturally and economically as digital citizens, they need to learn how to make informed use of technology, safely and responsibly, in order to contribute to wider society.

(Jisc RSCs, 2011)

In Chapters 7, 8 and 9 we will explore concepts of digital identities, citizenship and concerns around safety and responsibility.

Digital literacy in the curriculum

Definitions of digital literacy in FE and Skills sector curricula are not always immediately obvious, with the terminology having not completely filtered through to this level yet. However, you can find references to digital literacies within some curriculums if you look closely. The Functional Skills ICT curriculum is one such example. This curriculum lists skills such as the ability to 'use collaborative tools appropriately' and 'understand the need to stay safe and to respect others when using ICT-based communication' (Ofqual, 2011: 10–11) as key elements, both of which are key elements of digital literacy.

As the links between curriculum criteria and the need for digital literacy are not always made explicitly clear, it is important to remember that you as the teacher have the skills and creativity to design embedded activities and approaches to learning which allow for the use of digital tools, information and media to stimulate creativity, discussion and engaging learning experiences. This topic is covered further in Chapter 4.

As teachers in the FE and Skills sector, it is also important to be aware of how digital literacy is embedded into school curriculums. At Key Stages 3 and 4 (pupils aged 11–16), the new National Curriculum for Computing defines digitally literate pupils as being:

> *Able to use, and express themselves and develop their ideas through, information and communication technology – at a level suitable for the future workplace and as active participants in a digital world.*

> (DfE, 2013)

One of the key aims of this curriculum is 'to ensure all pupils… are responsible, competent, confident and creative users of information and communication technology' (ibid.).

This curriculum is designed for computing, but the digital literacy skills developed at this stage are designed to have a wider impact across the curriculum with the goal of creating digitally literate lifelong learners.

Activity

If you are currently teaching learners aged 14–16 years or 16–19 years consider how you can plan lessons which build upon the digital skills your learners will have learned at Key Stages 3 and 4. How can you ensure that your learners continue their digital skills development?

All the definitions explored so far frame the development of digital literacy skills in learners around being a 'good digital citizen'; that is being able to understand your rights and responsibilities, as well as your wider contribution to society when using digital devices, tools, social media, information and media. This 'real world' approach to learning skills is at the heart of how we teach in the FE and Skills sector: teachers using their industry and life experience to provide rich examples in learning environments, and encouraging learners to use their talents, skills, experiences and creativity to build a portfolio of their development. This in turn can have a positive effect on a learner's career prospects and choices.

Example

Jody is a 19-year-old learner of a Level 3 Extended Diploma in Media Make-up at her local college. She regularly posts photos of her make-up design work on Facebook and Instagram for her friends and family to see. She also re-pins photos of others' work she is inspired by on Pinterest. She recently organised a charity event in her home town which saw members of the public take part in applying make-up effects to raise money. Photos of the effects on participants were shared across social media networks and the hashtag #makeupformoney went viral. In the end over £1500 was raised for the charity.

As Jody's personal tutor you encourage her to collect all of this online evidence together in a blog, which she can then show to potential employers. With some support from you Jody sets up the blog and her creativity is unleashed. Inspired by her designs, charity work and enthusiasm she applies for and gets a placement with a media marketing company. She has since decided to study a similar subject at university.

Across the FE and Skills sector there is much diversity in terms of programmes, levels and learners, from 16 to 19 Study Programmes and Apprenticeships through to community-based adult education and Access to HE programmes. The sector serves, then, learners with a diverse range of abilities, expectations and backgrounds. Embedding the learning and development of digital literacy into programmes could be a great way of unleashing learner potential, creativity and enthusiasm, as well being an engaging method through which to approach wider issues and subjects. The FE and Skills sector, with its focus on skills, the needs of employers and the needs of the learner is arguably the best placed education sector in the UK for the excellent teaching of digital literacy to flourish.

Digital life skills and digital capabilities

'Digital life skills' is a term currently used in some parts of the FE and Skills sector to describe learning and teaching of the skills needed for the effective and inclusive use of ICTs and digital technologies. The term is referred to in the *Skills for Sustainable Growth* strategy policy document, published by the Department for Business, Innovation and Skills (BIS, 2010). In this document the importance of good teaching and learning about ICT and digital devices is referred to in terms of 'digital life skills'. The document states, in the context of 'supporting young people to make the transition from education to work', that:

Using a computer and the Internet are now basic skills for employability, and for many other aspects of learning and living.

(BIS, 2010)

This approach has been further bolstered by the release of the government's *Digital Inclusion Strategy* (Cabinet Office, 2014). This strategy sets the agenda for all public agencies to embrace digital inclusion and work towards the goal of educating all who can be, to be 'digitally capable' by 2020. This means that everyone has access to the Internet, is able to use digital services and has basic digital skills. This is split into three areas: 'connectivity', 'accessibility' and 'digital skills'.

Using this approach is allowing some services within the FE and Skills sector to target learning of ICT and digital skills to groups most likely to be excluded from digital technologies usage. This includes those identified as in danger of social exclusion through disability, unemployment or living within a deprived postcode area. It is now accepted that having access to the Internet and having the skills to use it well are key parts of living, learning, working and engaging with society in the twenty-first century. Therefore 'digital inclusion' is an important concept to understand as a teacher.

Understanding how learners could be digitally excluded and being able to identify the signs is vitally important. The subject of digital inclusion is further explored in Chapter 4.

Information and media literacies and critical thinking as elements of digital literacy

It is clear that the term 'digital literacy' has developed as our relationship with technology has changed, but it is also deeply rooted in the wider ideas of literacy that have been developing over the last fifty years.

Digital literacy was classified as one of many 'new literacies' by Lankshear and Knobel (2006: 16). These new literacies have evolved with the changes in Western societies through the later twentieth century and into the early twenty-first century. Lankshear and Knobel attribute the opportunities created during this period of post-industrialisation, such as rapid rises in social mobility and increased diversity in culture and language, as being the main underlying reason for the evolution of new literacies. In the same period technology advanced at such an unprecedented rate that new ways of communicating arguably developed and became necessary.

Among Lankshear and Knobel's (2006: 20) list of new literacies are 'information literacy' and 'media literacy'. These two terms are probably the most internationally established of the new literacies with a wealth of published research, theory and case studies available on them. In the UK, information literacy is a widely accepted and used term in education to describe the process people go through to understand their own needs for information, searching for it, accessing it, evaluating it and using it in an appropriate manner. Information literacy education is evident across education sectors in the UK, but there is sometimes the perception that these skills are only required for academic study in higher education.

In the FE and Skills sector the term 'information skills' has sometimes been used to describe information literacy learning in a vocational context, with teachers and librarians using real-life examples of how becoming information literate prepares you for researching job, career and training opportunities, allows you to be a lifelong learner, and ultimately, could help you to be more employable.

The term 'media literacy' has a similar meaning to information literacy, but it frames learning around identifying different types of audio, visual and text-based media and understanding the different approaches to 'reading' and using both. In the UK, media literacy is not a widely used term. However, it is accepted that in the digital age we need to understand 'multimodality' – that is, our abilities to communicate with and through, and to critically read, the range of audio, visual, text-based information we are presented with in digital environments.

Activity

What is your level of multimodality? Think about the following questions and then think how you can improve your capabilities with each:

- *Are you able to screen read, or do you print out digital text-based documents to read on paper? Can you use any digital tools to manipulate documents online rather than printing them off?*

- *Think about your abilities to identify key points and critically analyse arguments in text. Which methods do you use? Are you able to do the same when watching a video or listening to an audio clip? Which methods do you use in those circumstances?*

Critical thinking

One of the common themes across all the new literacies is critical thinking, and the knowledge, skills and support people need to do it well. This is not a new idea, with learning and teaching of critical thinking being a key part of the education debate since the publication of Paulo Freire's (1970) *Pedagogy of the Oppressed*. Freire's idea of changing the model of education, from one of teachers simply transferring knowledge, to one of learners being active participants in the creation of knowledge, has been highly influential.

The concepts of learners being 'co-producers' of knowledge and learning and active participants in their own education have become extremely popular in recent times, and the ability to think critically across situations and scenarios is vital to this working well. Critical thinking is vitally important whether consuming, producing and/or communicating in digital environments – as Starkey (2012: 54) puts it, critical thinking is at the heart of participation 'in a digital age society'. In making sure critical thinking is a key part of developing digital skills, we can take a more informed and confident approach to our digital technology usage.

Example

Richard is planning an assessment in which he wants his learners to work together in groups to research about new technologies and then present their findings back to the class. The external examiner has previously raised questions about the quality of student work with regards to plagiarism and over-reliance on limited sources of information, and Richard has noticed that the class are becoming bored with activities involving poster presentations. Richard decides to try to engage them by embedding creativity and critical thinking through use of digital tools. He splits the class into groups and gives them the choice of presentation method: Prezi, PowerPoint or Storify. They are required to find at least one of each of the following sources to help them

(Continued)

(Continued)

make their points: 1) a news article from the last twelve months; 2) a video clip; 3) a digital image; 4) a blog entry or tweet; and 5) information from an e-book. Included in the criteria for the assignment are the following:

- *You should assess the sources you are using based upon how up-to-date they are, the quality and trustworthiness of them, and record these details on the worksheet provided.*

- *Evidence of the sources you have used must be provided in the form of a list at the end of your assignment. This must list the Author, Date, Title and URL/website address of each of the sources you have used.*

- *While working on the assignment you should record your experiences of using different digital tools using a method you feel comfortable with (either written or audio recording is acceptable). Record how you felt at different stages, how easy/difficult different parts of the assignment are to complete and finally what you are learning as you work through the assignment.*

Richard knows that such an assessment is radically different from others they have been set before and decides to spend most of the first lesson going over the criteria and helping them to organise how they are going to approach it. Some learners are initially sceptical and struggle to engage, but these are balanced with those who see the task as an interesting challenge and actively want to engage. Richard gets them to explore digital tools and work out how to use them. He reminds the class that they have a lot of freedom to explore the Web and digital tools in this assignment and they should see it as a chance to bring into class some of the websites and tools they use outside college. By the end of the first lesson everyone is on task and engaging. By the end of the assignment, when they are presenting back it is obvious how engaged they have become in the task, with each one very proud of their finished product.

Digital literacy includes vital elements of information and media literacies and is concerned with how we make sense of, rationalise and critically think about our interactions with digital information, media, devices and tools. Digital literacy differs from information and media literacies in that it is concerned with how people produce as well as consume, and allows for the encouragement of creativity and innovation. Chapter 6 explores information literacy and critical approaches to using digital information and media.

The relationship between digital literacy and ICT skills

Learning and teaching in using computers, software and the Internet have been labelled IT and ICT education for many years. Terms like 'ICT skills' and 'basic computer skills' have become very loaded, with lots of different meanings and expectations having been built onto them, as people's needs from technology have evolved and changed.

Example from the author's own experience

My experiences of IT education make me realise how much people's needs from such courses have changed over time:

- *In the late 1990s I undertook a short CLAIT course at an FE College while studying my A Levels. The course was covered using computers for tasks relevant to everyday life and work, such as understanding the main features of a Microsoft Windows-based computer, using word-processing software to type and print letters and entering data into spreadsheets in order to produce graphs and charts. At the time we were told that skills in these packages were sufficient skills for most home and work-based tasks.*

- *By 2005, when I was running IT workshops for the public, there was very little interest in learning about word processing and spreadsheet software. Session attendees instead wanted to know how to set up and use email accounts, buy and sell on Ebay and how to upload and manipulate their digital photographs. This was a clear change, from people wanting IT training in order to computerise the paper-based tasks they did, to people wanting IT training to enable them to do new things and change their habits.*

- *In 2015, our needs for IT training have evolved and changed again, with people now wanting to know how to choose, set up and manage a variety of online accounts (e.g. social media accounts, cloud-based storage accounts and communication service accounts); advice on making decisions on which devices to purchase/discard and what benefits each has over the other (e.g. PCs, laptops, smartphones, tablets); to know how to present themselves professionally online and apply for jobs and other opportunities; help with linking together and managing all the digital devices in their home, in order to share files, music, photos and video with ease (e.g. WiFi routers, smart TVs, wireless printers, wireless audio systems).*

We now expect IT training to answer the question: 'how can I manage all aspects of my life through digital technologies?'

The question raised in the example above shows that a 'one size fits all' approach to IT training is no longer possible, as expectations of IT training are so diverse and person-specific.

It is therefore sensible to make a clear distinction between learning basic IT skills for functional usage and learning how to become knowledgeable and skilled in a world of digital technologies. This does not necessarily mean teaching the two ideas separately, but it does mean being able to give types of learning names and being able to better manage them when planning lessons, or even whole curriculums. Separating them into two different sets of ideas could look like this:

- **Functional IT skills** – the basic skills required to understanding and use key pieces of computing hardware and software. This could cover everyday usage through to usage in specific settings and for specific purposes. Learning these skills could involve learning anything from switching on a computer and using a mouse, to creating an email account, to setting up a wireless broadband router and connecting devices to it. These are skills which tend to be task or goal orientated.

- **Digital literacy skills** – the knowledge, skills, abilities, confidence and competencies required to develop our usage of digital technologies. Development of critical thinking, creativity, responsibility and productivity is facilitated and encouraged, allowing us to use digital technologies for living, learning and work.

Making a distinction between these two skills sets should not be seen as giving preference to one over the other. Both are equally important and should be understood and recognised as such. Taking the time to understand and unravel both skills sets could allow teachers to become more able and confident practitioners in skills sets which are undoubtedly essential for good learning and teaching.

Activity

Think about how the two skills sets, 'functional IT skills' and 'digital literacy skills', are embedded into curricula at your institution.

- *Which, if any, of these skills are you required to teach, and how comfortable do you feel in doing so?*

- *Are these identified as separate skills taught at a separate time from their subjects, or, are they embedded so that learners see them as transferable skills?*

Digital literacy skills and abilities

Definitions of digital literacy are useful as a starting point and for establishing the context, but a set of skills and abilities to structure your development around is vital if you are to make them work for you in your context.

When thinking about the actual skills of digital literacy, we should also consider the attributes, approaches and practices we want to develop. We have identified that there is no 'one size fits all' set of digital literacy skills and that it is more important to understand the scenario, the people involved and the desired outcomes for that person and the task they are engaged in. It is a good idea to first identify current needs, abilities and practices before developing yourself or others. Chapter 3 will help you to understand your current digital needs, abilities and practices, and Chapter 4 will enable you to consider those of your learners. Once you understand these conditions, models and frameworks of digital literacy should be used to guide development along a set of themes.

Many organisations in the UK have produced skills sets and frameworks for digital literacy. Cardiff University have produced a skills set of 'Learning Literacies', of which digital literacy is a key component, as part of their *Digidol Project* (Cardiff University, no date). This lists 'finding', 'managing', 'manipulating', 'developing/producing' and 'sharing' information as key processes of digital practice. They then break this down further into the digital 'attributes, practices, skills, access and awareness' of students.

Jisc (2014) identify 'seven elements of digital literacy' which could have a wide range of skills and practices associated with them. The seven elements are:

- Communications and collaboration
- Career and identity management
- ICT literacy
- Learning skills
- Digital scholarship
- Information literacy
- Media literacy.

The Jisc RSCs (2011) created an FE and Skills sector-specific model, using 'bubbles' of digitally literate practices, which take an issues and themes-based approach:

- Be safe in a digital environment.
- Find, evaluate and apply information.
- Use digital tools – hardware/software.
- Understand social responsibility.
- Showcase achievement.
- Awareness and management of digital identity.
- Collaborate – education, community and working life.

The BCS (2013b) have not produced a skills set as such but have chosen the following issues and themes as being key components of their definition of digital literacy:

- Understanding the impact of new technologies on society.
- Understanding and being able to manage digital identities appropriately.
- Being able to locate, organise, understand, evaluate, analyse and present digital information.

The approach to developing a set of digital literacy skills can either be based upon a set of processes a digitally literate person should/does follow, or be based around broader themes and issues with skills and practices developing in response. Both approaches can be useful when understanding how to develop yourself and your learners. For teachers in the FE and Skills sector it seems more appropriate to start with issues and themes and then develop practices, skills, knowledge and understanding around them.

From these various definitions, skills sets and approaches we can pick out common themes, attributes, skills, practices and behaviours of the digitally literate person (Table 2.1).

Table 2.1 A digitally literate person...

A digitally literate person is:

- Adaptable
- Creative
- Competent
- Confident
- Willing to learn
- Included
- Innovative
- Responsible
- Employable
- Knowledgeable
- A critical thinker
- Cultured
- Collaborative
- A citizen
- Analytical
- Expressive
- A learner
- A communicator
- Engaged
- Agile.

A digitally literate person does these things:

- Uses (digital tools and technology)
- Expresses themselves
- Develops (ideas)
- Participates actively
- Engages
- Collaborates
- Understands
- Contributes
- Thinks critically
- Creates/produces
- Stays safe
- Respects others

- Researches
- Shares
- Remixes/reuses
- Interacts
- Interprets
- Communicates
- Evaluates
- Publishes
- Edits
- Adapts/evolves
- Learns
- Speaks (types, communicates)
- Reads (words, media)
- Finds, searches and discovers
- Manages (information and media content)
- Multitasks.

A digitally literate person engages with digital technologies and digital skills for:

- Understanding/knowledge acquisition
- Self-improvement and development
- Their work
- Lifelong learning
- Development
- Living/life
- Inclusion in society
- Entertainment
- Continuous professional development
- Leisure
- Communication
- Business
- Creative expression
- Career prospects
- Engagement
- Democracy.

Activity

Look through the lists in Table 2.1. Pick out the words and phrases which describe how you currently operate in digital environments. Which other words and phrases would you want to work towards becoming? Are there other words you could add to the lists?

Each of us has a wide variety of interactions with technology and no two persons' experiences of the digital world are exactly the same. Therefore, the digital literacies a person needs and develops are context specific. For this reason there will always be differences in terminology, meaning and, ultimately, understanding of what is meant by certain skills depending upon who they were developed for. Digital literacy development does not exist in isolation. The literacies should be thought of as being transferable, interchangeable, remixable and updatable. Like digital technology itself, the skills are prone to upgrade as things change! With these thoughts in mind we can begin to understand how we as teachers can become digitally literate practitioners.

The digitally literate teacher framework

Most of the definitions and models of digital literacy focus on the skills needed by learners. This seems right, as we are all lifelong learners and as professionals are committed to professional development. However, we need to consider what digital literacy means specifically to teaching professionals, as it is about more than just our own learning. As teachers, we need to develop our understanding of digital information, media, software and devices for our own productivity, learning and development. We also though need to develop the confidence to facilitate learners in understanding their own digital practice and skills in using technology. As Beetham (2013: 37, citing Greener, 2009 and Yoo and Huang, 2011) identified, the confidence or anxiety teachers hold towards technology can greatly influence how learners use it and understand it.

Despite this assertion, the learning and development of digital literacy skills by teachers is currently quite fragmented, with different practice occurring in different training programmes and in different institutions. Traditionally, approaches to training teachers in technology have concentrated on the functional IT skills a teacher will need in the classroom. This has generally included teaching people how to use interactive whiteboards (IWBs) – e.g. SMART and Promethean boards – virtual learning environments (VLEs) – e.g. Moodle and Blackboard – and other information and learning technologies (ILTs), such as polling and voting systems – e.g. Turning Point – as well as learning resource systems. Very few teacher training programmes ask trainees to consider how they might develop and teach critical thinking and creativity with digital technologies. Those programmes which do cover these elements tend to be more specialist qualifications, considering learning theories and pedagogies in relation to digital and e-learning. It could be argued that learning of these principles is vital for all teacher trainees when digital technologies are such an integrated part of education.

Other vital elements of digital literacy for teachers, such as selecting digital content and apps based on pedagogical principles, dealing with issues of cyberbullying, digital safety and security, and teaching responsible digital citizenship, are identified by many teachers as training needs, but coverage of them is sometimes seen as a niche developmental need when problems arise, rather than an early teacher training need. All teachers in the FE and Skills sector need to understand these issues and many others if they are to become digitally literate and teach digital skills.

There are also a number of wider professional benefits to be gained from developing your digital literacy:

- Accessing current research and maybe even contributing to it.

- Discovering and using a wide range of freely available, but legal, digital content you can use with your learners.

- Engaging with subject and industry communities online.

- Sharing good practice and showcase your talents and skills online.

- Better management of your professional digital identity and learning how to use it to your advantage.

- Applying your understanding of your role and professional responsibilities effectively in digital environments.

- Reflecting using digital tools.

The following chapters will help you to think about and start doing the above. To aid you in your development, the following 'Digitally Literate FE and Skills Teacher Framework' is divided into seven strands of issues and themes. The following chapters will deal with these issues and themes and discuss how you can develop skills, practices, knowledge and understanding around them.

You are encouraged to edit/adapt this framework to best suit your needs, including adding or removing strands as appropriate. The strands presented here should be seen as a starting point, not an end in themselves.

The seven 'strands' of digital literacy Identified as being of importance to FE and Skills teachers are as follows. The digitally literate FE and Skills teacher:

- Understands their own position as a **digitally literate professional** and the **relationship between skills and practice**.

- Recognises the **digital needs, abilities and practice of learners** and plans **learning and teaching** around development of **relevant digital skills**.

- **Selects appropriate digital tools** and seeks to **use them creatively, critically and productively**.

- Develops a **critical approach to digital information and media** while becoming more **information literate**.

- Forms and manages a **professional digital identity** and uses it to **engage professionally**.

- Understands and leads on **digital safety, security, ethical and legal responsibilities and citizenship**.

- **Reflects critically** upon digital experiences and **plans for further development**.

Table 2.2 shows the seven strands with a description of each and links to coverage in the subsequent chapters.

Table 2.2 The digitally literate FE and Skills teacher framework

The seven strands of digital literacy	Description	Chapter covered in
1. Understands their own position as a digitally literate professional and the relationship between skills and practice.	Understands what digital practice means for professional teachers in the FE and Skills sector. Identifies the knowledge and skills required and is able to shape their own development around them.	3 and 10
1.1 Understands their own digital needs, abilities and practice, and plans for their own development.	Understands their own digital needs in relation to skills, practices, knowledge and understanding and capabilities, while adopting a set of digital principles. Looks at their current practice, as well as that of others and uses this to plan for their own development. Understands the debate around digital abilities and capabilities and recognises that everyone should be encouraged to develop functional IT skills and digitally literacy.	3 and 10
1.2 Understands the relationship between digital literacy and their subject area(s).	Understands the digital needs and demands of their own curriculum and subject area, as well as those of funding and regulatory bodies. Is able to use their digital literacy to embed appropriate digital learning.	4
2. Recognises learners' digital needs, abilities and practice, and plans learning around the development of relevant digital skills.	Understands the issues around learning in the digital age, digital exclusion/inclusion and equality of access. Understands learners' digital needs, abilities/skills, practices, knowledge and understanding. Considers this against other factors such as background, aspirations and general abilities. Takes this knowledge and uses it to inform teaching, learning and assessment.	4
3. Selects appropriate digital tools and seeks to use them creatively, critically and productively.	Identifies and understands the range of software (apps, digital tools, social media and services) and hardware (classroom technologies, mobile devices and specialist equipment) available.	5

(Continued)

Table 2.2 (Continued)

The seven strands of digital literacy	Description	Chapter covered in
3.1 Understands and uses digital technologies in professional practice creatively and critically.	Is willing and able to use digital technologies in professional practice, experimenting where appropriate, but recognising and observing best practices, legal, policy, safety and security concerns.	5
3.2 Teaches creatively with digital technologies and takes into account pedagogical concerns.	Embeds use of digital technologies into learning appropriately and encourages learner creativity through interactive and engaging activities. Understands the pedagogical theory around digital learning.	4 and 5
4. Develops a critical approach to digital information and media while becoming more information literate.	Understands the principles of information literacy and applies them to their professional practice and development, as well as learning and teaching. Can distinguish between different types of digital information and media and is able to search for, find, assess, use and apply digital information. Actively seeks out and discovers digital information in order to improve teaching practice.	6
5. Forms and manages a professional digital identity and uses it to engage professionally.		7
5.1 Forms and manages a professional digital identity.	Through the use of social networks and media and other digital tools, forms a positive professional digital identity. Critically understands and engages with issues of digital footprint, reputation and capital.	7
5.2 Contributes to, and engages in, digital communities in order to establish and maintain a digital identity.	Is an active creator/producer, sharer and curator of digital content/resources. This includes sharing achievements (e.g. participation in projects, successes, publications and outcomes), participation in online communities of practice and sharing of digital content. Understands significance of engagement in digital communities to non-virtual world.	7

The seven strands of digital literacy	Description	Chapter covered in
6. Understands and leads on digital safety, security, ethical and legal responsibilities, and citizenship.		8 and 9
6.1 Understands digital safety and security concerns, and is aware of safeguarding responsibilities and procedures.	Understands legal responsibilities to children and vulnerable adults as a teacher and applies this to own practice (e.g. cyberbullying, grooming and inappropriate conduct online). Understands how equality and diversity, and the related professional standards, legislation and local policies apply to digital environments.	8
6.2 Understands own legal, ethical and professional rights and responsibilities when using, creating and publishing digital content.	Understands the legal implications of using media and information from online sources and of publishing own content, including knowledge and application of copyright legislation, licensing and issues around plagiarism and acknowledgement of sources.	9
6.3 Understands the definition of digital citizenship and recognises the rights and responsibilities we each have in digital environments.	Understands how we are digital citizens with rights and responsibilities, and is able to develop own practice around this. Understands how actions online can have real-world significance.	8 and 9
7. Plans for continuous professional development (CPD) and tracks digital trends. Makes use of digital tools for reflection.	Reflects upon their own development of the other six strands and action plans for future development. Uses the insights and tools to monitor future digital trends and uses them to improve their own knowledge and skills. Is able to use appropriate digital tools to enable reflection.	10

Activity

Go to Appendix 1 to see the digitally literate teacher framework mapped against the sector professional standards. Use this to start thinking about your current level of digital literacy. In which areas do you need to focus your development?

Summary

In this chapter you have learned:

- How digital literacy is defined by key organisations and theorists.

- What digital literacy means in the context of the FE and Skills sector.

- How digital literacy relates to other literacies and critical thinking.

- The differences between ICT skills and digital literacy skills.

- What knowledge, skills and abilities a digitally literate teacher needs to have.

- About the digitally literate teacher framework used throughout this book.

In addition to this:

- Having completed the activities you should have put the fundamental concepts into context and have a basis on which to build your knowledge, understanding and skills as you progress through the rest of the book.

- You may have started to plan your own learning and development in the seven strands of digital literacy presented in the digitally literate teacher framework.

References and further reading

Anyangwe, E (2012) '20 ways of thinking about digital literacy in higher education', *Guardian Higher Education Network*, 15 May .Available at: http://www.theguardian.com/higher-education-network/blog/2012/may/15/digital-literacy-in-universities.

Bawden, D (2008) 'Origins and concepts of digital literacy', in C Lankshear and M Knobel (eds) *Digital Literacies – Concepts, Policies and Practices*. New York: Peter Lang Publishing, 17–32.

BCS (2013a) *BCS Digital Literacy for Life Programme*. Available at: http://dlfl.bcs.org/.

BCS (2013b) *More about Digital Literacy*. Available at: http://dlfl.bcs.org/content/ConWebDoc/50888.

Beetham, H (2013) 'Designing for active learning in technology-rich contexts', in H Beetham and R Sharpe (eds.) *Rethinking Pedagogy for a Digital Age*. 2nd edn. Abingdon: Routledge, 31–48.

BIS (2010) *Skills for Sustainable Growth – Strategy Document – Full Report*. Available at: https://www.gov.uk/government/uploads/system/uploads/attachment_data/file/32368/10-1274-skills-for-sustainable-growth-strategy.pdf.

Cabinet Office (2014) *Government Digital Inclusion Strategy.* Available at: https://www.gov.uk/ government/publications/government-digital-inclusion-strategy/government-digital-inclusion-strategy.

Cardiff University (no date) *Learning Literacies Framework.* Available at: http://digidol.cardiff.ac.uk/ learning-literacies-framework/.

DfE (2013) *National Curriculum in England: Computing Programmes of Study – Key Stages 3 and 4.* Available at: https://www.gov.uk/government/publications/national-curriculum-in-england-computing-programmes-of-study.

FELTAG (2013) *FELTAG Recommendations: Paths Forward to a Digital Future for Further Education and Skills.* Available at: http://feltag.org.uk/wp-content/uploads/2012/01/FELTAG-REPORT-FINAL.pdf.

Freire, P (1970) *Pedagogy of the Oppressed.* 30th Anniversary edn. Translated by M Bergman Ramos. London: Continuum.

Glenday, J (2013) 'Facebook claims daily active UK users now number 24m', *The Drum*, 14 August. Available at: http://www.thedrum.com/news/2013/08/14/facebook-claims-daily-active-uk-users-now-number-24m.

Holt, R (2013) 'Twitter in numbers', *Telegraph*, 21 March. Available at: http://www.telegraph.co.uk/ technology/twitter/9945505/Twitter-in-numbers.html.

Jisc RSCs (2011) *Digital Literacy – Organisational Review.* Available at: http://www.jiscrsc.ac.uk/ digitalliteracy/organisational-review.aspx#.

Jisc (2014) *Developing Digital Literacies.* Available at: http://www.jisc.ac.uk/guides/developing-digital-literacies.

Lankshear, C and Knobel, M (2006) *New Literacies: Everyday Practices and Classroom Learning.* 2nd edn. Maidenhead: Open University Press.

Ofcom (2014) *The Communications Market Report 2014.* Available at: http://stakeholders.ofcom.org.uk/ binaries/research/cmr/cmr14/2014_UK_CMR.pdf.

Ofqual (2011) *Functional Skills Criteria for ICT – Entry 1, Entry 2, Entry 3, Level 1 and Level 2.* Available at: http://www2.ofqual.gov.uk/downloads/category/68-functional-skills-subject-criteria.

SFA (2014) *Delivering Online Learning: SFA Response to FELTAG Report.* Available at: https://www.gov.uk/ government/publications/further-education-learning-technology-action-group-recommendations-sfa-response/delivering-online-learning-sfa-response-to-feltag-report#definition-10-wholly-online-component.

Starkey, L (2012) *Teaching and Learning in the Digital Age.* Abingdon: Routledge.

3   DEVELOPING YOUR DIGITAL PRACTICE

In this chapter you will learn:

- To consider theories of digital practice and apply them to your own development.
- About the assumptions and perceptions that are sometimes made about people's digital abilities and capabilities, and how these can hinder development.
- About the digital environments we use and how you can develop your interactions within them.
- About the principles you should use to guide your development as a digitally literate practitioner.
- How to work collaboratively to develop your digital literacy development and teach digital skills more effectively.

Links to the Digitally Literate FE and Skills Teacher Framework

1.   *Understands their own position as a digitally literate professional and the relationship between skills and practice.*

1.1   *Understands their own digital needs, abilities and practice, and plans for their own development.*

In Chapter 2 we explored what it means to develop as a digitally literate FE and Skills sector teacher and set out a developmental framework to use for this purpose. In this chapter, you will be asked to consider your current use of digital technologies and the interactions you have through them, and to identify how you build your development based upon this.

Digital practice

Digital practice is the study of how individuals and groups use and apply digital technologies to everyday tasks, learning and work, with many studies looking at the practice of learners/students with technology in particular. When considering professional teaching practice, we could observe many scenarios where digital technologies are used, or where a solution is needed for a digital problem, and then look to see how knowledge, skills and abilities are utilised, as well as the approach taken.

Two interesting models for examining digital practice have been put forward by White and LeCornu (2011) and Sharpe and Beetham (2010). White and LeCornu's (2011) approach is to better understand the digital practice of individuals by exploring their need for the Web and digital technologies and investigating how they approach their usage of it. Depending upon our needs and how we approach the Web, we are either 'visitors' to it or 'resident' upon it. Those who are visitors see the Web as a means to an end, rather than a social experience, and go to it with a specific task in mind. They find and use the appropriate digital tools and then leave. Those who are resident on the Web see it as a 'place' (ibid.) where they go to communicate and interact, use tools and share experiences. According to White and LeCornu (2011) individuals can move between being visitors and residents depending upon their engagement with the task in hand, and assert that we may change from being visitors to residents at different points. This movement could be seen as a developmental path where, as our engagement grows, so does our need for critical thinking around our usage. This could include understanding our rights and responsibilities in a digital environment and to keep ourselves safe and secure.

The ability we all have to develop and change our practice with digital technologies is also evident in Sharpe and Beetham's (2010: 90) model of students' usage of technologies. Their model is a pyramid containing four levels, each representing the level of engagement an individual has with digital technologies. At the bottom of the pyramid is 'functional access' to technologies, rising to two middle levels of 'skills' and 'practices', before reaching the top level, which is 'creative appropriation'. This model can be used to identify both needs and development goals (ibid.). At the top level, the individual's digital knowledge, understanding, skills and abilities have developed to the point that they are 'unconscious through practice' (p. 92). That is, they have taken full control of their own learning and development in relation to their use of/practice with a particular digital technology and they are able to manipulate and use the piece of technology appropriately and successfully for their needs. Beetham (2011) further developed this model into a literacies development framework for Jisc, where 'creative appropriation' is relabelled as 'attributes and identities'.

These approaches highlight the importance of understanding our own needs for using digital technologies and how we currently use them. From this point we can then begin to develop our knowledge, skills and engagement levels in order to move to becoming literate in our usage of them.

Activity

Think about how you use digital technologies in a professional capacity.

- *Which social networks, media, apps, tools and devices are you 'resident' upon and which do you occasionally 'visit'? Does this make a difference to how you use them? How critically engaged are you in each? Do you have more of a deeper understanding of those you are resident upon compared to those you visit?*

(Continued)

(Continued)

- *Take the technologies you use the most and think about Sharpe and Beetham's (2010) categories: functional access, skills and abilities, and creative appropriation. What would you need to learn, develop and achieve in order to progress from having functional access to them to being able to appropriate them creatively?*

Assumptions and perceptions

Assumptions are sometimes made about people's technological abilities and their capabilities to learn and develop them. These can be based upon the age, background, experiences, perceived intelligence and aspirations of a person. There are obvious dangers in relying upon such assumptions as predictors of abilities and capabilities to learn them, which could lead to the destruction of confidence within that person, or their exclusion from the digital age.

One such assumption has become a commonly held and widely accepted belief in education: that younger generations are inherently more digitally aware, knowledgeable, skilled and capable in their use and understanding of technology than older generations.

This idea was given credence by two articles written by Marc Prensky in 2001 (2001a; 2001b). In these articles he coined the phrase 'digital natives' to describe young learners who were children, teenagers and those of typical undergraduate age at the time. This group is labelled as 'Generation Y', and subsequent 'digitally native' generations are 'Generation A' and 'Millennials'. Prensky stated that this generation was the first to be '"native speakers" of the digital language of computers, video games and the Internet' (2001a: 1), as they had been immersed in technology from an early age. A range of examples from neurology and psychology are cited by Prensky to develop a theory that learners from this generation had brains which had developed to work and move between types of multimedia and digital environments much quicker than previous generations and processed information in a different way (2001b).

At the time of publication of Prensky's articles, the majority of teachers would have been born between the 1940s and 1970s, in the 'Baby Boomer' and 'Generation X' generations. Prensky categorised those from these generations as being 'digital immigrants', who did not share the digital abilities, understanding and practice of 'Generation Y', and whose brains had developed to learn, work and consume information and media in an 'analogue' way (2001a; 2001b). This, according to Prensky, meant that there was a big difference between the expectations and abilities of learners and those of their teachers, and he asserted that 'today's students are no longer the people our educational system was designed to teach' (2001a; 2001b).

This set of ideas has had powerful resonance ever since, with many asserting them as fact and using them as a basis for training and development, as well as to influence learning and teaching experiences.

To take Prensky's ideas and categorise people so definitely is an extremely simplistic approach to a far more complex picture of knowledge, skills, abilities and capabilities. Bennett *et al.* (2008) and McKenzie (2007) have reviewed the debate around 'digital natives' and 'digital immigrants' and have concluded that little to no evidence supports the under-lying claims. In fact, to counter these claims, Bennett *et al.* (2008) cite a wide variety of research showing that development of cognitive abilities, such as those required to mul-titask effectively, vary between individuals due to a wide variety of factors, with date of birth not being key. Younger generations are no different from others in having a range of socioeconomic, lifestyle, health, behavioural and confidence factors which can have affected their development of skills, abilities, attitudes and capabilities. Over-simplistic labelling of people can be counterproductive to providing an inclusive environment where everyone is empowered to learn new skills and utilise new methods.

The FE and Skills sector is diverse and draws people to teach from a wide variety of back-grounds, age groups and from a wide variety of industry sectors and subject specialisms. Within that mix there will be teachers with varying degrees of confidence, experience, knowledge and skills in using digital technologies, and the level to which a person partici-pates in digital interactions does not necessarily equate to them having a deep understanding of their usage and being completely digitally literate.

Regardless of your starting point, you should concentrate on developing your digital liter-acy based upon your individual needs, and see this as a developmental journey. You should take the same approach when teaching and supporting learners and colleagues in their digital development too.

The digital environments we use

We find ourselves learning, teaching, playing and working in a variety of different digital places, spaces and environments and through a variety of different devices. In terms of places, spaces and environments this can include, but is not limited to:

- **Open environments** (such as social networks/media, discussion forums/boards and anywhere else freely accessible on the Web) – the content can be seen, shared, com-mented upon by anyone.

- **Closed/restricted environments** (such as groups, networks and media where mem-bership is by invite only or is shared with only a selected community/audience. Parts of virtual learning environments (VLEs), such as group work activities, can be thought of in this way) – the content is only available to invited or registered users.

- **Private/personal environments** (such as email accounts, personal storage in the cloud, personal areas of institutional portals and VLEs) – the environment and its con-tent is only available to you. You may be able to customise the environment and possibly communicate or share some content with others through it.

The digital environments we find ourselves interacting within may differ depending upon a range of factors. For example, we may make choices based upon:

- The task

- Our likes and preferences

- Our confidence and comfort levels

- The design and user experience of the environment

- Security and safety concerns

- Ethical and legal concerns

- Our professional responsibilities and identity.

Our choices may also be bound by constraints and restrictions such as device limitations, peer pressure/popularity of an environment, organisational restrictions and preferences or the availability of the information, the media or the digital tool itself. It is important to consider these reasons, as by thinking more critically about the environments we choose and use we are able to think towards making informed choices. It is also important to consider that learners may have reasons, including some of those mentioned above, as to why they may or may not use, or want to use, particular digital environments.

Activity

- *Consider some of the factors listed above. Do you have preferences for particular types of digital environments? Do you think about any of those factors and actively make informed choices?*

- *Think about some of the digital environments you use in a work context (including any you use informally, e.g. to communicate about work). How many of them are the results of you making an active choice and how many others are decided for you? What are the potential security, safety, ethical, legal and professional responsibilities you need to consider when using each environment? Is there anything you should do differently?*

Developing our digital interactions

Thinking about the digital environments we interact within only allows us to understand one part of our digital practice – that is, where we use digital technologies. What we do within these environments is also key. Digital technologies can be used in a wide variety of ways, depending upon the purpose we have in mind at that particular moment, our intended aims and outcomes, or the associated activities we decide to participate in.

Example

You may want to use a digital technology to listen to a song, read a document or watch a video clip. The reason for doing this could be singular or it could be an activity which is part of a wider goal. Listening, reading and watching may only be the first step before we give feedback as a comment or write a review. You may then share the media and your comments upon it via email or a social network. You may decide that you want to edit the original and use a part of it for a new project.

The interactions mentioned in the above example can be split into four categories:

- **Consumption.** This includes the acts of watching, reading, listening and viewing. In isolation, this is quite a passive experience.

- **Comment.** This could be everything from a 'like', a 'favourite', through to a text-based response, such as a review. This is a participatory experience.

- **Communication.** This can be audio, video or text based. It is a participatory experience. It can be two way between friends in a private/personal environment, or could take place between many users in an open environment. A comment-based activity could lead to conversation.

- **Creation.** This involves creating or editing, and then publishing and sharing a piece of digital content or software. It will probably also involve a combination of the other categories. This is a highly participatory experience.

Most users of connected technology are digital consumers first and foremost, and a lot of people also combine these activities with communication and comment, but a relatively smaller number go on to create multimedia and digital products. It is often thought then, that the most common activities undertaken in digital environments are more passive than participatory. However, any interaction can be turned from being 'something we just do' passively to an activity in which we critically engage. This can be seen when we consume something with the desire to learn from it or act upon it. As we watch, read, listen and view, we are absorbing knowledge and ideas. This involves interpretation, analysis, evaluation, forming opinions, generating ideas and planning. We might also be consuming from the digital world to take and use in the physical world.

Example: using YouTube

Claire has never considered YouTube to be a learning tool. Her children watch videos on it a lot and she has watched many with them, mostly short 'funnies' involving pets behaving like humans. Her children and their friends are always sharing links to these videos, and Claire has had to set a limit on the amount of time they are allowed to spend on YouTube each day. Claire is surprised then, when an email from the school asks parents to watch a video on YouTube with their children about the dangers of strangers. Claire watches the video and notices that it has been uploaded by a children's charity. This makes Claire realise that YouTube and other online video services could be useful for much more than just entertainment. Claire is a manager and teacher at a centre for adult learners. She searches within YouTube for videos on a couple of topics they are currently planning to deliver and discovers a range of videos. She watches four and of those, three are suitable, as they are of good quality, of the right level for the learners, are quite engaging and have been uploaded by a UK-based educational charity she knows of and trusts. The fourth she discards, as it looks too old and the last couple of minutes have a commercial subtexts and appear be trying to sell a product.

(Continued)

(Continued)

Intrigued, she takes the name of the account which uploaded the video and types it into a search engine. This search reveals that the name is of a company which supplies learning software packages, many of which have unverifiable claims about their benefits. Claire decides to show the videos to her team and engage them in a discussion of how they could use them to engage their learners. Claire wants to find a way for the learners to have an activity to do after the videos, so that they are not just watching but are also thinking and applying.

In the example above, Claire's digital interaction is solely consumption, but she is definitely an active participant in the experience. She is exercising many cognitive processes: she has concern for her children's time utilisation and development; her approach is open, collaborative and creative, as she identifies opportunities to improve her professional practice, embed teamwork and increase engagement with learners; she uses critical judgement to make informed choices. There will be multiple impacts of this activity in the physical world.

Given the nature of digital environments, undertaking one type of interaction or activity very often leads on to others and this very often happens as a natural progression rather than as a giant leap. In the example of Claire, she could try the other three interactions as a natural progression following her initial activities. For example, she could comment by writing a constructive response to a video in the comments box below it, and she could combine this with communication by sharing the video to a social network, such as Facebook and Twitter with a comment. She could further communicate by contacting the creator of the video through YouTube to let them know how she has used the video. As she grows in confidence and gains more experience she could create digital content by submitting lesson materials and activities to a repository, such as TES Resources. Going further, she may consider setting up a professional blog, and could write a reflective account of her experience as her first post.

Activity

Think about the activities you currently undertake in digital environments and the types of interaction these involve.

- *Which of the categories of interaction do you engage with the most: Consumption, Comment, Communication or Creation?*

- *If there are any interactions you rarely or never have, what course of action will you take to experience them, learn them and develop in them?*

- *How engaged do you feel you are in your digital interactions? Would you consider yourself critical, creative, responsible and professional in your approach to them? Are there any activities you undertake where you need to become more engaged in considering your interactions?*

Principles to guide your digital practice

So far, we have considered where we do things in digital environments, what interactions we have within them, and have looked at putting digital abilities into a developmental context.

Being a critical thinker, making informed choices and being creative are central to everything covered so far and are key to becoming a digitally literate practitioner. As a part of this it is important to understand and apply a set of key principles to the interactions you have with digital technologies. The principles set out below have evolved and developed to be central to the ethos of an 'Internet for all' and for a digital world which serves the needs of the physical world, as well as for its own advancement. The principles are:

- Criticality
- Creativity
- Responsibility
- Inclusivity
- Openness
- Collaboration.

Throughout the chapters in this book, the theory, methods and practical examples are all underpinned by these principles and you will frequently be reminded to consider them. Let us consider what we mean by each of these principles.

Criticality

What is it?
Critical thinking was discussed in Chapter 2 as being the basis for the formation of most new literacies, including digital literacy. The abilities to read critically and to analyse and assess digital sources of information, multimedia, apps, tools and social media for such factors as authenticity, accuracy and safety are vital to empower good decision-making when so much is available instantly.

How is it important to FE and Skills sector practice?
Critical thinking is an important skill to develop. As a teacher and practitioner it allows you to make informed decisions when using or planning to use digital technologies, multimedia and information. It allows you to use your professional judgement and to justify an approach.

Do you do it?
Think about when you are planning lessons which involve delivery through technology or activities and assessments requiring learners to use technology or research for digital information and multimedia. Do you critically think about the learning outcomes of a digital approach when planning? Do you consider factors such as safety, security, data ownership and accuracy when selecting apps, social media, digital tools and mobile devices for learners to use? When setting activities and assessments involving research of information and multimedia, are you clear in your guidance to learners on how to undertake research and do you set clear criteria on how they should evaluate and assess what they find? Chapters 5 and 6 explore these processes in more depth.

Creativity

What is it?

The principle of creativity is that everyone should be given opportunities, skills, encouragement and the right environment to imagine, think, experiment, play and ultimately produce a product (which could be anything from a piece of writing to a piece of software). John Howkins (2009) states that anyone can be creative if the conditions and the environment are right, and undoubtedly this involves providing a safe environment in which to get things wrong and fail and also to focus, channel and use the creativity generated to enhance learning and development. It involves active participation and collaboration in learning and teaching and what Anna Craft (2011: 19) refers to as a 'democratic' and 'enabling' approach to education. When combined with the other principles, and primarily criticality, it can make for a powerful approach to learning and teaching.

How is it important to FE and Skills sector practice?

The 'creative industries' are extremely important for jobs and skills and according to figures published by UK government in January 2014 (DCMS, 2014) they form the fastest growing industrial sector of the UK economy. Fostering digital creativity through our practice will certainly help learners to prepare for jobs in these industries, but creativity is not only associated with the 'creative industries'. It is actually an attribute that is highly sought after in most industries. Howkins (2009: 25), drawing upon research conducted in the UK by Peter Higgs and others from 2008, points out that over half of those who consider their work to be creative are not employed in the creative industries. If we think in terms of the careers we are preparing our learners for there are a great many situations and scenarios where creativity is a necessity. For example, if learners are entrepreneurial and want to start and run a business, won't they need to be creative in their ideas and vision?

Do you do it?

Think about your delivery approach to new topics and theory. Do you mostly deliver this presentation or 'chalk and talk' style or do you involve learners in the process of building knowledge and learning new concepts? When setting activities, do you choose methods which allow learners to work together and use their imaginations and experiment? Do you give learners opportunities to design, make and create things, perhaps using digital tools? In the next chapter we will explore further digital approaches to learning and teaching which embrace creativity.

Responsibility

What is it?

Whether we are consuming, commenting, communicating and/or producing in digital environments we have societal, ethical and legal responsibilities. These can be around how to use and reuse digital content fairly and within licensing and copyright restrictions, being aware of the issues around online defamation and understanding what may be classed as bullying and discriminatory behaviour online. It also includes taking responsibility for our own actions and also for safeguarding.

How is it important to FE and Skills sector practice?

Understanding our legal, professional and ethical responsibilities with regards to how we interact as teachers in digital environments, and to how we safeguard, protect and educate our learners about being responsible in digital environments, is a vitally important part of professional practice. Chapters 8 and 9 look at how we can understand, approach and deal with these issues.

Do you do it?
Think about the following questions: have you ever had to teach any of these topics to learners? Think about how you approached it. Do you see dealing with responsibilities in digital environments as an area you need to understand and teach? Have you ever had to deal with an incident of cyberbullying? Do you know what legal and ethical responsibilities you have to copyright and licence holders when finding and using information and multimedia?

Inclusivity

What is it?
Inclusivity in a digital context is the principle that all are included and are able to participate. Steps are actively taken by those with authority and power, such as communications providers, providers of education and individual teachers, to encourage and enable the participation of all. It is of key importance that everyone is digitally included in an age where accessing services, learning and employment opportunities depend upon access to the Internet and basic digital skills.

How is it important to FE and Skills sector practice?
Digital inclusion is a key responsibility of the FE and Skills sector, as the sector works with those in danger of exclusion. This can include those not in education, employment or training (NEETs), those from lower social economic backgrounds and those with little or no interest in getting online and using technology.

Do you do it?
Depending on which part of the FE and Skills sector you work in, you may or may not have experience of being part of a digital inclusion agenda. If you do not, the principle is still an important one that all FE and Skills teachers should be aware of. Are you aware of whether any of your learners are digitally excluded? Would you know what to look for and how to help? Chapter 4 explores this principle in more detail and provides guidance.

Openness

What is it?
As the use and power of the Web has grown over the last decade to reach more people and connect them, so have various movements to 'open' up data, information, knowledge and learning. The principle is to increase and encourage mass participation in education without the barriers of physical access and large cost. As an educational principle, openness allows us to question practices and beliefs held since before the digital age such as: Are physical spaces needed in which to learn and teach? What role(s) should the teacher play: facilitator, navigator, leader, content creator? Do the 'best' sources of information always cost money?

How is it important to FE and Skills sector practice?
The opportunities and challenges that the principle of 'openness' poses to the FE and Skills sector should not be underestimated. Massive open online courses, or MOOCs, as they

are commonly referred to, are courses and modules studied completely online through digital instruction and/or resources. The idea is that they are provided completely free to learners and anyone with an Internet connection can participate. The main debate about MOOCs has been, until recently, focused upon higher education and universities, but it is now accepted that the target audience for MOOCs is those who would normally participate in lifelong learning and adult education courses (Clark, 2014) and some MOOCs are being aimed at GCSE and A Level students (Parr, 2013). Therefore the FE and Skills sector is definitely at the centre of the open learning movement. Chapter 4 explores how you can utilise the principles of open learning and MOOCs in your practice.

Open education resources (OERs) are an older, but still very important, part of the open learning movement. The idea behind OERs is that digital resources, materials and objects created by teachers are shared and exchanged online. Chapters 6 and 7 explore finding, using and participating in OER networks.

The Open Access (OA) movement is concerned with making publicly owned and funded data, information, research findings, and media freely accessible to all. Chapter 6 further explores OA resources and Chapter 9 explores rights and responsibilities when using and sharing OA materials, including copyright and licensing considerations.

Do you do it?
Think about your approach to learning and teaching, your professional development and your own learning. Are you open minded to new approaches, methods and ways of working? Do you believe that learning and knowledge should be free? Whatever your answers to these questions at this stage, you should be able to develop your understanding of the openness principle as your progress through the book. Remember, embracing this principle does not mean sacrificing others, and we must be as critical of new methods as we would be of any others.

Collaboration

What is it?
The principle of collaboration is to work with others to achieve objectives, to share knowledge, ideas and experiences and to utilise each other's skills and abilities. This aligns particularly well with the principle of openness. This could involve collaboration in digital environments and through digital technologies, or through collaboration with colleagues and contacts.

How is it important to FE and Skills sector practice?
Collaboration can be extremely useful in our practice when learning and teaching digital skills, as it can reduce individual workloads, and utilise the skills and abilities of a range of staff effectively. The FE and Skills sector employs people with a wide range of skills abilities relevant to the different strand of digital literacy. The section below explores how we can develop our approach to collaborative practice.

Do you do it?
Work through the next section, which explores collaborative practices, and undertake the activities in order to answer this question.

Activity

Look at the principles and their meanings above.

- *Are these principles a part of your digital practice (as a teacher, as a learner, or any other part of your professional practice)?*

- *Which appear to be the most immediately relevant to your practice, and which do you want to investigate more?*

Working collaboratively on digital practice

Becoming a digitally literate practitioner could involve learning many new skills, understanding new concepts, and sometimes adapting and changing practices. This can be quite a daunting practice, which if not managed carefully, could lead to unnecessary stress and extra work.

Becoming digitally literate does not mean that you should try to become an expert in absolutely all areas of digital technologies. Instead, you are encouraged to identify knowledge and skills gaps and form strategies for development. In order to make this more achievable the principles of collaboration and openness (mentioned above) can be embraced to enable team work with colleagues. By doing this you could:

- Develop and learn together

- Share knowledge, ideas, expertise and best practice

- Improve learning and teaching

- Build relationships and understanding between teams.

Starkey (2012) asserts that educational institutions have become complex environments with a wide variety of different 'actors' (staff) all involved in making parts of the institution work and function. In an FE and Skills sector institution these 'actors' could be a wide range of staff, with varying expertise in different areas. The following staff may be employed by your institution, or you may have access to them via service-level agreements with other institutions or organisations. These professional support colleagues exist to support you and your learners, so making links with them can be extremely beneficial:

- **Librarians and learning resources staff.** These members of staff work on a day-to-day basis with digital information resources and multimedia for learning and teaching purposes. If they are qualified librarians they will have a thorough understanding of information literacy and research skills. They may currently offer and provide teaching and support to learners on topics associated with information literacy, and in some cases other topics of digital literacy, such as keeping safe online and promoting a positive image online.

- **Careers and guidance professionals.** These members of staff are qualified to work with learners on the development of their career and job-seeking abilities and to provide guidance in identifying the most suitable careers. In the digital age, professionals in this area are aware of a wide range of suitable digital sources of information and multimedia for career planning, and can provide support and teaching to learners on areas of digital literacy through an employability lens.

- **Personal tutors/mentors.** The people responsible for personal tutoring and mentoring vary by organisation, but the responsibilities they have are broadly the same. Academic and pastoral is usually offered with topics around aspects of citizenship, rights and responsibilities, ethical and legal concerns and study skills high on the agenda.

- **Information technology (IT) equipment and network professionals.** These members of staff are often responsible for setting policies around usage of an organisation's IT equipment, the IT network and access to the Internet. They may also have responsibility for or be part of the development of social networking guidelines/policies and lists of digital tools, apps and services acceptable for staff use.

- **Information and learning technology (ILT) experts and learning technologists.** Unfortunately, not every organisation employs these members of staff, but where they do exist make use of them! They can help you to understand digital environments for learning and to make informed decisions about using classroom technology, VLEs, digital tools, apps, services, mobile devices and social media. Increasingly, they are also taking on the wider agenda of leading on digital literacy. If this role does not exist within your organisation, you can contact Jisc, through their website, for support and advice.

Activity

Getting started on team development of digital literacy.

- *Gather together your immediate colleagues to discuss the digitally literate teacher framework, each other's digital practice and the digital principles.*

- *Work together to identify knowledge, skills, good practice and expertise, as well as knowledge and skills gaps, within the team and decide on an approach to support each other's development.*

- *Invite colleagues from the professional support teams listed above to your next meeting to discuss the knowledge and skills gaps within your team and to discuss how they can support your learning and teaching.*

Summary

Activity

Having read Chapters 2 and 3, write a statement about each of the following:

- *What digital literacy means for you in the context of your own practice.*
- *To what level you currently feel confident in your abilities as a digital practitioner.*
- *What you are going to do in the short term to increase your confidence and abilities.*

In this chapter you have learned:

- To consider theories of digital practice and apply them to your own development.
- About the assumptions and perceptions that are sometimes made about people's digital abilities and capabilities, and how these can hinder development.
- About the digital environments we use and how you can develop your interactions within them.
- About the principles you should use to guide your development as a digitally literate practitioner.
- How to work collaboratively to develop your digital literacy development and teach digital skills more effectively.

References and further reading

Beetham, H (2011) *Literacies Development Framework*. Available at: http://jiscdesignstudio.pbworks. com/w/page/46740204/Digital%20literacy%20framework.

Bennett, S, Maton, K and Kervin, L (2008) 'The "digital natives" debate: a critical review of the evidence', *British Journal of Educational Technology*, 39(5): 775–86. DOI: 10.1111/j.1467-8535.2007.00793.x.

Clark, D (2014) 'MOOCs have burst out of higher education into vocational learning. VOOCs have arrived', *TES FE Opinion*. 21 February. Available at: http://news.tes.co.uk/further-education/b/opinion/2014/02/21/39-moocs-have-burst-out-of-higher-education-into-vocational-learning-voocs-have-arrived-39.aspx.

Craft, A (2011) *Creativity and Educational Futures: Learning in a Digital Age*. Stoke on Trent: Trentham Books Ltd.

DCMS (2014) 'Creative industries worth £8 million an hour to UK economy' (press release). Available at: https://www.gov.uk/government/news/creative-industries-worth-8million-an-hour-to-uk-economy.

Howkins, J (2009) *Creative Ecologies: Where Thinking is a Proper Job*. London: Transaction Publishers.

McKenzie, J (2007) 'Digital nativism, digital delusions, and digital deprivation,' *From Now On: The Educational Technology Journal*, 17 (2). Available at: http://www.fno.org/nov07/nativism.html.

Parr, C (2013) 'FE colleges "may lose students to Moocs"', *Times Higher Education*. 9 May. Available at: http://www.timeshighereducation.co.uk/news/fe-colleges-may-lose-students-to-moocs/2003709. article.

Prensky, M (2001a) 'Digital natives, digital immigrants', *On the horizon*, 9(5). Available at: http://www. marcprensky.com/writing/Prensky%20-%20Digital%20Natives,%20Digital%20Immigrants%20-%20 Part1.pdf.

Prensky, M (2001b) 'Digital natives, digital immigrants, part II: do they really think differently?', *On the horizon*, 9(6). Available at: http://www.marcprensky.com/writing/Prensky%20-%20Digital%20 Natives,%20Digital%20Immigrants%20-%20Part2.pdf.

Sharpe, R and Beetham, H (2010) 'Understanding students' uses of technology for learning: towards creative appropriation', in R Sharpe *et al.* (eds.) *Rethinking Learning for a Digital Age: How Learners are Shaping their own Experiences*. Abingdon: Routledge, 85–99.

Starkey, L (2012) *Teaching and Learning in the Digital Age*. Abingdon: Routledge.

White, D S and LeCornu, A (2011) 'Visitors and residents: a new typology for online engagement', *First Monday*, 16(9). Available at: http://firstmonday.org/ojs/index.php/fm/article/view/3171/3049#p4.

4 ASSESSING AND RESPONDING TO DIGITAL NEEDS

In this chapter you will learn:

- What digital needs are and the factors you need to consider around them.
- What digital inclusion is and how you can shape your practice to ensure all learners are able to access and develop digital skills.
- Strategies for engaging learners in understanding and developing their digital skills, in line with curriculum and subject area needs.
- About pedagogical approaches with digital technologies and digital skills.
- What 'open' learning is and how it is relevant to the FE and Skills sector.

Links to the Digitally Literate FE and Skills Teacher Framework

1.2   *Understands the relationship between digital literacy and subject area(s).*

2.   *Recognises learners' digital needs, abilities and practice, and plans learning around the development of relevant digital skills.*

3.2   *Teaches creatively with digital technologies and takes into account pedagogical concerns.*

What are digital needs?

Regardless of how and why we currently use digital technologies, we all have digital needs. These may either be needs that we recognise, understand and are taking steps to fulfil, or they may be needs which are not immediately obvious, are not recognised and not understood by an individual. They may also be denied, not prioritised or misunderstood by the individual. As teachers, it is our responsibility to not only recognise our own digital needs, but also to help learners recognise their own digital needs, and provides and promote opportunities for them to learn digital skills.

Examples

Mark has worked as a skilled manual labourer since leaving school. Now in his late 40s, he realised a couple of years ago that by not using computers and the Internet and having very limited skills in doing so, he was missing job opportunities, did not have the skills to progress to the jobs he wanted to do and was not part of some of the social interactions his friends and family were having online. To overcome these barriers he purchased a tablet PC and, with the help of friends, began to get online and started using social networks and job websites. Mark has reached the limit of what he can learn informally and has enrolled on a short course at his local FE college. He hopes that this will enable him to learn more about office applications and using the Web more productively. He hopes that by gaining skills, experience and an IT qualification, he will feel more confident and able to apply for supervisory-level jobs within his industry. Eventually, he may study further for management qualifications. During the IT course, one of Mark's friends tells him that a lot of people within the industry are finding out about jobs by networking on social networks. The friend tells him to put his CV online. Mark decides to ask his teacher if anyone at the college can help him with this. Mark has recognised how learning digital skills may help him achieve his goals and is taking steps to fulfil his digital needs.

Sophie has never used the Internet and has only tried using a computer once, but found the experience confusing and difficult. This was due to there being a lot of information to take in and understand and the person instructing her was going too fast and became impatient and frustrated when she made slow progress and did not understand. As a result, Sophie decided that computers were 'not for her' and that she could get everything she needed without one. She has been defensive over the years about not using computers and is proud of what she has managed to do without them. After spending many years working as a hairdresser, Sophie has recently enrolled on a barbering course at her local FE college to learn extra skills and potentially grow her client base. Since joining the course, she has been surprised by how much technology is available in the college and how much is used by the teacher in-class. She was at first happy, as the course did not appear to require her to use technology, as most of the work was paper based, but she recently discovered that they will have to sit a computerised test and is secretly scared of not being able to do it. She is too scared to ask for help, as all the other students are happy to do this and appear very able in using technology. During an in-class discussion about using social networks and media to promote salon businesses and make connections with clients, and using specialist salon software to manage bookings, Sophie became annoyed at what she saw as 'being a waste of time' and irrelevant to the course. Later, when the teacher got out the laptops for everyone to type up their handwritten client sheets, Sophie became angry and left the room, feeling that the course is not for her after all and that it was a mistake to waste time and money on it when she could carry on doing her current job without needing to use computers. Sophie is suffering from a lack of confidence and fear about technology and this is leading to anger and denial of the need to learn new skills. She does not understand how learning digital skills could help her and what her digital needs are.

Activity

Read the two case studies above and consider how you could help and support both Mark and Sophie. Consider the following:

- *Mark is making progress, but needs to be sent in the right direction. Who could help him within your institution and how?*

- *Sophie is considering leaving college, and if she does, the experience may stop her from accessing learning opportunities in the future. How could you ensure that she continues, recognise and support her needs, and convince her of the need to learn digital skills?*

The two examples above highlight how learners may feel about using digital technologies and learning digital skills. Learners may have a diverse range of reasons for wanting to learn digital skills, or barriers stopping them from being able to learn them. The role of the teacher enables them to identify these goals and barriers, and helps learners to make good choices about their development.

Chapter 3 discussed the debate around people's capabilities to learn to use digital technologies and, as was discussed, assumptions should not be made based upon people's ages and backgrounds. Instead we must look at the individuals' needs for digital technology and base skills learning around this. Changes brought about by technology in the digital age mean that there is now a need, and arguably a right, for everyone to have basic digital skills, and access to them, so that they can engage in the following:

- **Communication** – digital devices and apps are becoming the main method of communication for some people, and some people may only be reachable via these means in the near future. Digital communication enables many more options for keeping in touch, such as instant messaging and video chat.

- **Opportunities** – those with Internet access have the means to find more job and career opportunities and can apply for them more quickly and efficiently.

- **Public services** – many public services are becoming easier to access online and some services are likely to go completely digital in the near future. The UK Government is driving forward plans to make available all public services, which can be, online.

- **Shopping and access to the best prices** – many products and services are cheaper to purchase online and some may be only available digitally in the near future. Many people shop around for the best price when purchasing more expensive products and services, using price comparison websites.

As FE and Skills teachers we therefore need to consider how far we are able to ensure that access to digital skills learning is offered and encouraged to all learners.

Thinking about digital inclusion

This is for everyone

Tim Berners Lee, the inventor of the World Wide Web, tweeted this declaration about the WWW during the 2012 London Olympics opening ceremony (in Berners Lee, 2012)

In considering learners' digital needs, we are starting to think about how we can include everyone in learning digital skills and how this is an important and developing role for FE and Skills sector teachers. These ideas fit under the term 'digital inclusion', which is the policy of enabling everyone to be able to access the Internet, digital technologies and digital skills through the creation of the necessary infrastructure and support. This then enables equality of access and opportunities in the digital age, to communication, access to learning and work opportunities, and vital public services.

Those without digital access and skills are digitally excluded, or are in danger of being digitally excluded, and it is therefore important that these groups are identified and seen as priorities for intervention. This inclusive approach is already deeply embedded into the FE and Skills sector, as IT and digital skills classes have been offered to all age groups for many years, and the sector's role in working with socially disadvantaged or excluded client groups is well established.

Strategic guidance in achieving the goal of universal digital inclusion has been provided by the UK government's Digital Inclusion Strategy (Cabinet Office, 2014). This strategy, with its focus on access to the Internet, skills and abilities, understanding the positive reasons to use the Internet and learning to trust the Internet, has set the challenge and mission to all public agencies to embrace digital inclusion and work towards the goal of educating all who can be, to be 'digitally capable' by 2020. Those in low paid employment, in poverty, in old age, past offenders, those in social housing, and any combination of these factors are the people most likely to be digitally excluded according to Ofcom (2013).

If we accept that working towards the goal of digital inclusion is a vital role for the FE and Skills sector, we must next consider how we can identify those who are digitally excluded or at risk of being. There is currently a digital divide within the UK between those who have digital access, knowledge, understanding and skills and those who do not, with those in the lowest socioeconomic band, C2DEs, having lower digital confidence scores than those in the highest band, ABC1s (Ofcom, 2014). This is interesting, as the lower socio-economic bands are big client group for the FE and Skills sector.

The digital confidence scoring system, which produces a digital quotient number, was developed through research by Ofcom (2014). This test ascertains participants' knowledge of, awareness of and attitude towards 'newer [digital] products and services', and produces a score at the end. With one hundred being the average score, Ofcom found that those aged under 44 are more likely to score above average, with 14–15-year-olds having the highest score in this age group. Those aged over 45 begin to decrease in their confidence score to around an average of eighty. These results do not necessarily show that a younger person is more likely to have any innate abilities in using digital technologies, but they are certainly more likely to be more confident in using them/attempting to use them. This shows that with both groups, care, attention and patience will be needed when encouraging them to use digital technologies in an efficient, safe and productive way. This may take the form of encouraging a younger learner to temper their overly-confident approach by applying critical thought, while an older learner may need encouragement to explore and creatively use technologies in order to overcome their fear. However, there will be many exceptions to the rule and we should not assume before we have asked. See the activity below for details of how you can take the digital confidence test, and perhaps even give it to your learners to do.

Activity

Search online for Ofcom's digital quotient test and get your score. The test consists of a short series of questions which seek to ascertain your knowledge and awareness of digital technologies and your attitude towards them.

- *Is your score above or below 100?*

- *What can you do now to increase your score?*

- *If you had your learners take this test how could you support them in understanding and developing their knowledge, understanding and skills based upon their results, whether high or low?*

Activity

Think about how you could help and support a digitally excluded learner.

- *Find out where they can access the Internet for free and what support is available in their community. UK Online Centres provide this access and support, and you can search to find the nearest one on their website here: http://www.ukonlinecentres.com/about-us/centre-search#/. These tend to be in public libraries, community centres, colleges and schools and are available across the UK.*

- *Identify courses and support services in your own college that can help learners get online, learn digital skills, navigate the Web and use digital services. Basic IT skills courses may be available and departments such as student services, learning resource centres and careers services can usually help.*

- *How can you make sure that learners feel supported and are engaged when you are using digital technologies in the classroom? Think about strategies you could put in place, before reading on to the next section of this chapter.*

Engaging learners in digital skills learning

If digital needs and digital inclusion are to be addressed, all learners need to be given opportunities to learn digital skills and to become digitally literate at a level appropriate to them. The form that this takes and the methods you use to teach these skills may be dictated by a range of factors, including:

- The level your learners are working at.

- The focus of the curriculum and your institution.

- The destinations of your learners after they complete the programme.

- The current digital practice of your learners.

It is therefore difficult to prescribe a 'level' to which all learners in the FE and Skills sector should reach with their digital skills. However, it is important that you identify opportunities to teach and foster digital skills at a level appropriate to your learners, so that they gain confidence in using digital technologies, make use of them for learning and work, and can start to engage more deeply with them on a critical and creative level. As this process is based upon your professional judgement of the factors listed above, you should choose whether it is appropriate to use terms such as 'digital skills' and 'digital literacy' with your learners or not, and when it is appropriate to give them a digital literacy framework to develop against.

Activity

How should you engage your learners in digital literacy development planning? Consider the factors listed above and ask yourself critical questions about each, such as:

- *Is development planning and reflection appropriate at this level?*

- *Could your learners use a personal development plan/portfolio in digital literacy to help them find a job? Enhance their career prospects? Progress to a higher level of learning?*

- *Are they interested in digital technologies to the point where some recognition of their knowledge, skills and abilities would benefit them?*

However you decide to teach digital skills and facilitate digital literacy learning, you should consider the following starting points about engagement with these subjects:

- **Plan to engage and include all learners.** As has been discussed, your learners may or may not be engaged in learning digital skills, depending upon a wide range of factors. Therefore you need to discover their digital needs (see earlier in this chapter) and plan learning of digital skills and use of digital technologies around them.

- **Do not teach negatively and from a 'fear' perspective.** Prohibition and fear do not tend to work very well as a teaching method, as they are dictatorial, rather than inclusive and they do not allow for creativity and critical thinking. The arguments of the previous decade about whether digital devices, tools and media have a place in education and whether they should be banned from the classroom have been superseded by the realisation that digital technologies are used in just about every aspect of modern life for a wide range of purposes. To exclude them from being a part of the learning process is to ignore the benefits of using them. A prohibitive approach could hinder the learning of vital digital skills and reduce opportunities for learners. Instead think about taking learners from the point they are currently working at in their use of digital technologies, to a higher level where they can see their development. Teaching from a positive perspective about digital technology use can lead to extremely interesting classroom discussions and improve the knowledge and skills of all participants, including the teacher.

- **Focus on transferable skills, not individual systems.** There are a variety of systems used throughout the FE and Skills sector, such as virtual learning environments (VLEs), library databases, e-book and e-resource systems, as well as productivity applications, such as word processors and presentation software. These systems should all be seen as a means to end, through the use of which transferable skills can be acquired and learning can take place. Placing the emphasis on these transferable skills will make the benefits of using them more apparent. Work through the next section of this chapter to think about the underlying pedagogical approach you are taking and use Chapter 5 to consider activities you could use.

- **Teach digital skills in context and use real-life examples and scenarios.** Some learners react with genuine surprise when they see that digital technologies have a place in education and some feel that their digital environments are purely personal and irrelevant to their programme of study. This is not helped if the teaching of these technologies feels removed from the learning objectives, or like an 'add on'. It is far better to embed the learning of digital skills into the curriculum and relate them to the subject being studied, or to real-life scenarios learners may face in the workplace.

- **Do not make assumptions.** As discussed earlier in this chapter and the previous about how age is no indicator of knowledge, skills and abilities with digital technologies. Therefore, we must teach the learners in front of us at a level appropriate to their needs and understanding.

Activity

Think about a module or unit you are currently teaching.

- *Are any of the following elements appropriate to the content of the curriculum:*
  - *Activities to design and create content or a product (using any combination of text, image, audio or video)?*
  - *Researching for information (either independently or group-work based)?*
  - *Communication (either to or with the group through presentation, or externally through work placement, or marketing and promotion)?*
  - *Learning subject knowledge and theory?*

(Continued)

(Continued)

- *Which digital technologies would be of use to learn and teach these scenarios?*

- *How could you embed the learning of digital skills into the usage of these technologies (use the digital literacy frameworks from Chapter 2 to help if necessary).*

- *How could you guide your students to use the technologies creatively, critically, professionally, ethically and safely?*

- *How could you build in a mechanism for learners to reflect upon their development of digital skills during these activities?*

Pedagogical approaches to digital technology usage and digital skills learning

Many FE and Skills sector institutions have invested heavily in digital technologies over the past decade, leading to a range of devices and systems available for teachers to use inside and outside of the classroom. This includes hardware such as PCs and laptops, mobile devices and tablet PCs, digital still and video cameras, as well as software such as virtual learning environments (VLEs), digital library resources and systems (e.g. e-books, e-journals and multimedia collections) and a range of other applications and tools. There is also a plethora of other software and media available for free online, such as apps, digital tools, information resources, audio and video collections, which are being utilised by teachers every day. The opportunities for learners and teachers to use these technologies and learn a wide range of digital skills cannot be underestimated, and we shall explore how you can start to use some individual technologies in Chapter 5. In this section though, we will explore the developing theories and methods around educational use of digital technologies for learning and teaching in order to form a theoretical underpinning to our digital practice and teaching of digital skills. This section is designed to give an overview of pedagogical approaches to digital technologies and skills that will help you consider the basics and form a base for critical thinking. For more in-depth discussion of pedagogical approaches to digital education you may want to read *Using Social Media in the Classroom* by Poore (2013) and *Rethinking Pedagogy for a Digital Age* edited by Beetham and Sharpe (2013).

The debate about the impact digital technologies have on learning and teaching has been the subject of debate for many years, with conflicting evidence on both sides. What is certain through, is that the presence of these technologies, and the truly innovative ways in which teachers and learners have used them, has 'disrupted' traditional learning and teaching methods and has opened up a wave of exciting experimentation that looks set to continue. With the right application of pedagogy to practice digital technologies can be used to:

- Better engage learners in taking control of their learning.

- Engage learners to critically think and to demonstrate and showcase their creativity.

- Design and deliver more diverse and interactive activities and learning experiences.

- Make more efficient and productive use of class time by changing the delivery of subject knowledge and theory.

This section will explore how we can use pedagogy to ensure these elements all happen.

When we look at pedagogical theory around using digital technologies and digital skills learning, we can identify the following categories to which theory and methods are applied:

- **E-learning and distance learning.** This involves learners taking courses online using materials, resources and assessments packaged for use in an online learning environment by teachers. Communication between teacher and student is usually by email, phone call or instant messaging. The course can be the same as is taught on-campus, or could be bespoke to the needs of an organisation or body.

- **Classroom-based learning, using digital technologies.** This is face-to-face learning within an FE and Skills classroom using digital tools, devices and resources in a physical environment. In the FE and Skills sector the 'classroom' could take many forms including a lab, workshop, studio, salon or workplace.

- **Blended learning.** This is when learners are on a course which utilises both e-learning and classroom-based instruction. This approach is quite popular in the FE and Skills sector, especially with apprenticeship courses and those tailored to employer need.

- **Open learning.** This type of learning is entirely digital, being initiated, undertaken and completed online. As this is an important and emerging area, it is covered in the section after this one.

Activity

Which of the above categories have you experienced as a teacher? Think about what approach you took to teaching:

- *Were you mostly giving them content and instructing them to take particular approaches, or were the learners involved in producing content and creating knowledge?*

- *Which approach(es) allow for the most critical thinking?*

- *Which approach(es) enable the learning of a range of digital skills?*

Regardless of which of the above categories your teaching fits into, if you are using digital technology you will be utilising one or more of the pedagogical approaches shown in Table 4.1.

Table 4.1 Pedagogical approaches

Method	Example	
Rote/didactic learning	Teacher controls the learning objectives, gives instructions, provides content and students interact with this by listening and making notes. Assessment is usually by test or exam.	Didactic pedagogy
Guided/resource-based learning	Teacher provides resources, materials which are used by learners to learn the subject in a set way. This could be individually or in groups. The teacher is still very much in control.	
Active learning	Learners are set activities which allow them to discover and gain a more personal and deeper understanding of the theory, concepts and ideas. Teacher is a facilitator and expert who is there to set some boundaries, support learners and check understanding.	
Experiential learning	Learners and teachers are equal partners in the learning process, but teachers do not necessarily need to be present at all. Knowledge is added to, created and discovered by the learners as they work through the subject, in other words by experience. Learners are extremely engaged.	Constructivist and connectivist pedagogies

No one method is right or wrong and, depending upon the needs of your learners and curriculum, you may need to employ a mixture of didactic and constructivist/connectivist methods. At their extremes and if not used appropriately, didactic, constructivist and connectivist methods can be the polar opposites of each other: didactic methods can be too rigid and not take into account the abilities, progression and needs of learners; and constructivist methods can become unfocused and unclear, and be too much influenced by the bias and limited experiences of the learners. If their use is based on learner and curriculum needs then they can be extremely effective, engaging learners and allowing them to gain a thorough understanding of a subject.

For the purposes of learning and teaching around digital technologies and skills, it is generally agreed by authors and theorists of the subject that constructivist approaches, which allow for much more creativity and critical thinking to take place and place learners at the centre of the learning process, are the most desirable, with Starkey (2012: 92) stating that 'in the digital age teachers will prioritise student learning over teaching', and Beetham, Sharpe and others (2013) using this approach to design digital learning approaches. In the next chapter we will look at creating learning resources, content and activities using digital tools, and will again pick up on the pedagogical aspects of doing so.

The following are approaches to learning and teaching that have gained prominence in recent years as methods to utilise digital technologies in the classroom:

- Flipped learning

- M-learning (mobile learning)

- Co-production of knowledge

- Digital storytelling and content curation

- Collaborative teaching

- Digital discovery learning

- Digital content creation

- Gamification.

These methods utilise digital technologies to put learners at the centre of learning and lean more towards the constructivist end of the pedagogical spectrum. Not all of them will be suitable for your learners, but it is worth researching each one and deciding if your learners will respond to it.

Spotlight on ... flipped learning

Flipped learning is the idea that material which would normally be delivered 'lecture' style in the classroom is delivered online as learning resources through the VLE for learners to watch before class time. This then allows class time to be used for more active and experiential learning. This allows learners to consolidate the theory side of the subject with the experience of 'doing it'. What would traditionally have been seen as class-time learning and homework learning are essentially flipped. Hence, flipped learning is also referred to as 'the flipped classroom'.

For teachers, they can monitor who is using the learning resources (which could be video and audio clips, worksheets and exercises, tasks and activities, lecture recordings, or interactive learning objects) with statistics from the VLE and the marking of work set and, importantly, spend more time supporting and helping learners, assessing their understanding and development, and working with them.

Find out more about this technique by watching the YouTube video of flipped classroom innovator, Aaron Sams, discussing and demonstrating the technique (techsmith.com, 2010) and by reading through the infographic on the Forbes website (Gobry, 2012).

Activity

Research each of the above learning and teaching approaches to find out what they are, how they work, examples and case studies of how they have been used, and consider how you might use them in your practice.

If you are struggling with your research, see Chapter 6 for help in developing an information literate approach.

Open learning – a disruptive force?

The term 'disruptive technologies' is sometimes used to describe situations where the development of digital technologies has led to big changes within an industry or the obsolescence of methods and accepted ways of doing things in a relatively short space of time. The most obvious example is the music industry, where the business model that had worked so well for over fifty years and had created a multi-billion dollar industry was made obsolete in the late 1990s with the invention of the digital music file (MP3) and the widely available means to freely create them from CDs and share them across the Internet. This meant that only a small number of people needed to buy the music, share it online and everyone else could download and keep it for free. The music industry's reaction to this was to turn to the law enforcement agencies to enforce copyright laws, close down music-sharing networks and take members of the public to court. For the industry this was both a public relations fiasco, an expensive failed attempt to hold on to a dying business model, and a missed opportunity to change their business model. Public relations fiasco, because many saw the court cases as David and Goliath battles; failed attempt, because the laws around copyright and piracy were not made to cope with this situation and could not always be used to stop music sharing; and missed opportunity, because the idea of easy to access and free at the point of use music had struck a chord with the public and many saw this as the way they wanted to obtain and listen to music, but with no legal means to do this, a music 'blackmarket' operated. Eventually, after a few years, the industry did catch up with consumer opinion and need, and embraced digitally available music, but the failure to adapt more quickly cost the industry many jobs, a lot of money and a lot of the revere and respect the public once had for it. The question that some are asking is whether adult education, both further and higher education, is about to have its 'music industry moment'.

The answer is unclear, as the adult education sectors serve a wide range of clients with varied needs, and a 'one size fits all' approach is never going to be suitable to all learners and for all courses and subjects. However, the relatively quick rise of open approaches to learning should not be ignored, and as a digitally literate teacher, it is important to understand them and consider if and how you could learn more about them and make use of them.

We have already looked at how you can use ideas like 'the flipped classroom' and utilise blended and e-learning approaches in the classroom, but open learning takes learning out of the classroom completely and transfers learning environments into the digital world.

Ideas and notions of 'educational institutions', 'teacher', 'learning resources', 'assessments' and 'qualifications' are being challenged and redefined by the evolution of open learning and some are beginning to question if the educational institutions, structures and methods we have today will continue to be relevant and required in the future.

The development and popularity of massive open online courses (MOOCs), which allow potentially thousands of people to simultaneously undertake a course in a digital environment for free, have taken the world of education by storm. Initially, it was thought that MOOCs would compete with only higher education (HE), but evidence suggests that a large proportion of those taking part in MOOCs are older learners wanting to learn additional skills and participate in short courses (Clark, 2014) rather than participate in degree-level courses and credit-bearing modules. This has led to interest in if and how the FE and Skills sector can use MOOCs to reach this group, who are a potential clients. The University for Industry (UfI) have therefore experimented in creating vocational open online courses (VOOCs) for the FE and Skills sector (Clark, 2014). The perceived benefits that MOOCs and VOOCs could bring to the sector include reaching those who would not access formal education through an institution such as a college, but who are digitally engaged and who could potentially be reached through their computers, tablet PCs and mobile phones.

Spotlight on ... MOOCs

MOOCs can be found on the Web, covering a wide range of subjects, mostly in short-course form. MOOCs can be classified into two forms:

- *__MOOCs run by organisations__ such as Khan Academy, Coursera, FutureLearn, Udacity and iTunes U are structured and organised with learners creating an account and 'signing up' for a particular course or module. Learning resources, such as video, audio, articles and chapters are then provided through a digital platform and learners choose when and where they access the materials and complete the assessments (if they are provided). The type of learning is mostly study based, with a didactic approach to the content, but some do feature interactive elements, such as interaction through instant messaging and commenting. Learners may also be required to work in virtual groups. This type of MOOC is being referred to as an 'xMOOC' (Kernohan, 2013; McGill, 2013).*

- *__MOOCs that are more free-form in nature__, with less of an emphasis on particular platforms and systems, instead using existing platforms, such as social networks to build learning communities, and networks also exist. These are more about sharing and co-producing knowledge and content and, therefore, the learning outcomes for participants are not set in stone. This type of MOOC is being referred to as a 'cMOOC' (Kernohan, 2013; McGill, 2013).*

Most of the MOOCs which have achieved attention have been of the xMOOC variety.

Due to the nature of MOOCs being about self-directed learning, and therefore requiring significant commitment and self-motivation, they will not be suitable for everyone. The modules and courses covered can also be quite specific and niche, and so may be more suitable for professionals topping up their knowledge, rather than those wanting to learn basic skills or study a fully rounded course. However, MOOCs are at an early stage and their full potential is yet to be realised. They may then be more fully utilised by the FE and Skills sector over the next decade. The UK government is already starting to consider how they can be regulated and funded in FE and Skills policy (Department for Education, 2013).

Activity

Take a look at the websites of some of the MOOC platforms, such as FutureLearn, Coursera, Khan Academy and iTunes U (the URLs can be found in the 'Links to digital tools, resources and systems' section in Appendix 2).

- *What do you think the perceived attraction and benefits might be to a learner?*

- *What disadvantages might there be over undertaking a course at an FE and Skills institution?*

- *Are any MOOC courses relevant to your practice and development? Could you undertake one to gain a better understanding?*

- *Could you use any of the principles of MOOC-based learning in your teaching practice? If so, how could you convince others of the benefits?*

Summary

In this chapter you have learned:

- What digital needs are and the factors you need to consider around them.

- What digital inclusion is and how you can shape your practice to ensure all learners are able to access and develop digital skills.

- Strategies for engaging learners in understanding and developing their digital skills, in line with curriculum and subject area needs.

- About pedagogical approaches with digital technologies and digital skills.

- What 'open' learning is and how it is relevant to the FE and Skills sector.

References and further reading

Beetham, H and Sharpe, R (eds) (2013) *Rethinking Pedagogy for a Digital Age: Designing for 21st-century Learning.* 2nd edn. Abingdon: Routledge.

Berners-Lee, T (2012) [Tweet]. 27 July, 2:08pm. Available at: https://twitter.com/timberners_lee/status/228960085672599552.

Cabinet Office (2014) *Government Digital Inclusion Strategy*. Available at: https://www.gov.uk/
government/publications/government-digital-inclusion-strategy/government-digital-inclusion-strategy.

Clark, D (2014) 'MOOCs have burst out of higher education into vocational learning. VOOCs
have arrived', *TES FE Opinion*. Available at: http://news.tes.co.uk/further-education/b/
opinion/2014/02/21/39-moocs-have-burst-out-of-higher-education-into-vocational-learning-voocs-
have-arrived-39.aspx.

Department for Education (2013) *16–19 Accountability Consultation*. Available at: https://www.gov.
uk/government/uploads/system/uploads/attachment_data/file/365980/16-19_Accountability_
Consultation_Document.pdf.

Gobry, P E (2012) 'What is the flipped classroom model and why is it amazing? (with infographic)',
Forbes, 11 December. Available at: http://www.forbes.com/sites/pascalemmanuelgobry/2012/12/11/
what-is-the-flipped-classroom-model-and-why-is-it-amazing-with-infographic/.

Kernohan, D (2013) 'Making sense of MOOCs', in JISC Inform, (36). Available at: http://www.jisc.ac.uk/
inform/inform36/MakingSenseOfMOOCs.html#.VLwgYIGQGrX.

McGill, L (2013) *UKOER Synthesis and Evaluation – Open Courses*. Available at: https://oersynth.
pbworks.com/w/page/63860065/OPEN-COURSES.

Ofcom (2013) *The Communications Market Report 2013*. Available at: http://stakeholders.ofcom.org.uk/
binaries/research/cmr/cmr13/2013_UK_CMR.pdf.

Ofcom (2014) *The Communications Market Report 2014*. Available at: http://stakeholders.ofcom.org.uk/
binaries/research/cmr/cmr14/2014_UK_CMR.pdf.

Poore, M (2013) *Using Social Media in the Classroom: A Best Practice Guide*. London: Sage.

Starkey, L (2012) *Teaching and Learning in the Digital Age*. Abingdon: Routledge.

techsmith.com (2010) *The Flipped Classroom*. Available at: https://youtu.be/2H4RkudFzlc.

5 SELECTING AND USING DIGITAL TOOLS

In this chapter you will learn:

- What is meant by the term 'digital tools'.
- How to approach the selection of digital tools for professional purposes.
- How to select and use digital tools to be a more productive professional.
- How to select and use digital tools to design and deliver learning and teaching.
- About your own usage of digital tools and their relationship with your creative talents.

Links to the Digitally Literate FE and Skills Teacher Framework

3.   Selects appropriate digital tools and seeks to use them creatively, critically and productively.

3.1   Understands and uses digital technologies in professional practice creatively and critically.

3.2   Teaches creatively with digital technologies and takes into account pedagogical concerns.

In this chapter, we explore how we can develop our own best practice around the selection and usage of digital tools for a range of purposes relevant to the work of the FE and Skills sector teacher. Building upon the ideas explored in Chapters 3 and 4, we shall consider how our knowledge and skills with digital tools can improve our digital practice and interactions in digital environments, as well as considering the best ways to select and use digital tools to ensure the needs of learners, our subject and our institution are met.

What are digital tools?

Throughout this book the term 'digital technologies' is used to refer to all Internet-connected hardware, software and Web-based technologies. The term 'digital tools' is used here to refer to the use of digital technologies in the pursuit of specific aims and objectives, or to achieve a specific function. This goes beyond simple consumption. When thought of in this way, any digital technology could be utilised as a tool.

This could include:

- **Free and open source software (FOSS)** – specifically, audio, video and image editors and learning object creation tools.

- **Cloud-based software and solutions** – specifically, office and productivity tools, and file storage.

- **Mobile devices** – such as smartphones, tablet PCs, cameras and recording devices.

- **Smartphone and tablet apps** – specifically, apps which facilitate the creation, editing and production of media and content.

- **Classroom technology equipment** – such as interactive whiteboards (IWBs), specialist equipment and other devices.

- **Digital content repositories, players and editors**.

- **Social tools** – such as blogs, wikis, social networks and social media-sharing tools.

Spotlight on ... the evolution of digital tools

From the creation of the World Wide Web in 1991 by Tim Berners-Lee through to the mid-2000s, most digital content, such as information and media, could be found on websites and in web pages published in Hypertext Mark-up Language (HTML). This content was intended, for the most part, to be consumed on a desktop PC through a Web browser (such as Microsoft Internet Explorer). Contributing to the Web was done by a relatively small number of people who were engaged enough to create their own websites. This involved learning technical knowledge and skills in scripting HTML in order to do the basics, and further skills were required in specialist software standards (such as Flash and Java) in order to create and upload multimedia content. The costs of purchasing space on the Web and a Uniform Resource Locator (URL), known as Web-hosting and domain name, were also prohibitive.

By the mid-2000s an evolution of the Web had started to take place. The technologies and tools had developed to the point where easy-to-learn and use Web services and tools allowed ordinary people to contribute and upload content to the Web, and create and edit content. The new technologies also enabled Web-based applications to communicate with each other, sharing data and carrying out tasks in the background which greatly improved the Web user's experience and led to the highly personalised digital environments we have today. This development of Web technologies and experience in the mid-2000s is seen by many to be the pivotal point when the Web became accessible, useful and indispensable to people and organisations, and our relationship with it changed fundamentally.

(Continued)

(Continued)

An evolution of technologies has led to a revolution in how we carry out everyday tasks and live our lives.

This social and technological evolution of the Web was labelled 'Web 2.0' by influential technology writer and publisher Tim O'Reilly (2005). In the article he observed that the Web is evolving to become a 'platform' on to which services and applications are built and exist, that data collected automatically from the preferences and contributions of users flows between these services and applications and that user-generated knowledge and content are taking precedence over the formally published in search engine results (O'Reilly, 2005). This all forms a Web that is collaborative, open to all, while at the same time being personalisable. The Web has moved far beyond something we access only on desktop PCs. We now use a wide range of devices to access the Internet and have the evolved Web experience through a wide range of digital technologies. This means the right tool is available whenever we need it.

For an overview of the technologies which underpin the Web see this Wikipedia article linked timeline showing how Web technologies have evolved: http://www.evolutionoftheweb.com/

Selecting and using digital tools

Whenever we start using a new digital technology, we are asked to read very lengthy 'terms and conditions' of usage documents and are sometimes presented with a short tutorial of how to get started. Very often there will be an instruction manual or help and support website available to view later. In reality though, some people watch the tutorial, fewer people use the instructions and help features, and very few read the terms and conditions of usage.

The lack of engagement with terms and conditions documents is unsurprising, as many of them are written in inaccessible legal language, and mostly say similar things. There are a few points you should look out for though, if you are going to use them as tools in your professional practice:

- What data is collected and stored by the technology?

- Do you (the user) retain ownership of your data, files and other content, or does it become the property of the company providing the technology?

- Do they list safeguards they have in place against data theft, hacks and data loss?

These questions become more important as the confidentiality and sensitivity of digital data and information increase, and the value of digital content increases.

Activity

Look at this list of approaches people take when first using a digital technology. Which of them do you currently do, and which do you need to start doing?

- *Investigate*

- *Play*

- *Use*

- *Understand*

- *Critically analyse/evaluate/apply judgement*

- *Respect/critically apply ethics*

- *Reflect on your approach*

- *Innovate.*

When selecting appropriate digital tools, we first need to think about the tasks we are undertaking and the outcomes we are trying to achieve. From this point, we can then start to think about factors specific to the situation and context, our needs of the tool, and consider advantages and disadvantages of one tool over another. By doing this you will be more critically engaged with the process of making decisions about your digital tool usage, and may even develop set criteria to analyse and evaluate the tools you are going to use. In Chapter 6 we look at specific criteria to use when evaluating digital information and media which may help you to think about the criteria you need to develop for evaluating tools across a variety of contexts. Throughout this chapter, criteria will be discussed for the main purposes FE and Skills teachers need in order to select and use digital tools.

Example

Olu and Amanda are going to be working collaboratively on a regular basis in order to produce reports, which will eventually go to the senior management team of their institution. However, they work at different campuses and there is very little crossover time in their hours. Amanda suggests that they use a cloud-based option, which will allow them to write the report together online without having to continually upload and download files. They will also be able to leave notes and comments for each other within the documents. There is also the benefit for Olu that this will be more convenient to him, as he predominantly uses a tablet PC. They decide that they will need to use the following types of digital tools:

(Continued)

(Continued)

- *A cloud-based storage option (with the ability to share files between multiple users).*

- *A cloud-based word-processing package (with the ability for multiple users to add comments).*

- *Email (to stay in touch).*

- *Tablet PC and apps (Olu works mainly from a tablet, so the cloud-based software they use will need to work through a tablet's Web browser, or ideally have an app available).*

- *Desktop PC and Web browser (Amanda works solely from a desktop PC, so the cloud-based software they use should work fine through a browser. However, Amanda will have to test which browser is most appropriate).*

Both Olu and Amanda are concerned about the nature of the information contained within the reports, as they include sensitive details about learner progress. Olu suggests that they should evaluate a range of tools before deciding, based upon the tools' security features, trustworthiness, ease of use, in-built options and features, and overall suitability to the task.

Selecting digital tools to become a productive professional

The tools we use to be productive have become more mobile and personal in recent years. Due to mobile devices, such as smartphones and tablet PCs, becoming viable alternatives to desktop PCs and laptops, we are now able to carry the following productivity tools with us wherever we go:

- **Calendars and diaries**.

- **Professional and work communication tools** – such as video conferencing, email and instant messaging.

- **Office applications** – such as word processing, spreadsheets, note taking and file storage.

- **Organisers and task planners** – such as 'to-do' lists.

- **Teaching and assessment tools** – in particular, presentation tools, assessment submission software and virtual learning environments.

- **Professional development and research tools** – such as reflection tools, journal and e-book databases.

The landscape of the available tools has completely changed over the last decade. Many free apps, cloud-based software and open access resources are now viable alternatives to the expensive software, hardware and resources that institutions and individuals previously had to purchase at considerable cost.

As productivity tools have gone mobile and personal, they have changed our relationship with work, professionalism, our colleagues and students. We are now able to do the following, regardless of our location and the time of the day:

- Access files and edit documents in the cloud.

- Work using mobile devices such as tablet PCs and smartphones.

- Communicate via email, instant messaging and video conferencing while on the go.

- Research using the Web, apps and online databases.

- Make and record notes, and organise them.

- Plan and organise our time and appointments with our calendar/diary.

- Collaborate on projects efficiently.

- Record our thoughts and reflections.

However, the increased accessibility and availability of productivity tools do not necessarily make us more efficient and productive. It could even be argued that increased exposure to work through digital tools could lead to overload, an uneven work–life balance and a blurring of the boundaries between work and home spaces. It is extremely easy for digital solutions to productivity problems to become the problems themselves, with evidence starting to emerge that addiction to digital technologies could be a real problem. A study of smartphone usage by psychologists Pearson and Hussain (2015) revealed that 13 per cent of the study's participants could be classified as being addicted to their smartphones, and these participants showed high levels of narcissistic and neurotic behaviour, possibly leading to poor psychological health and wellbeing. In her book, *Digital Dieting*, Tara Brabazon (2013) discusses the effect of our connection with digital technologies on our abilities to learn, teach and be productive professionals. Brabazon, uses push email as an example (this is where email is automatically received by a mobile device and the user is alerted to view it) to show that digital devices can end up determining 'work behaviour and patterns' (p. 5), rather than actually aiding the user to be more productive. This is due to the fact that services like push email continue to run inside and outside working hours. Brabazon also noted, quoting a *Guardian* journalist, Ian Price, that those using push email on these devices spent two and half times more outside working hours on work emails.

If over-exposure to mobile digital devices could actually be detrimental to health and our personal lives, then it is extremely important to select productivity tools with care and manage them so that they work for you, make effective use of your time and enable you to switch off when you need non-work time.

Following these simple steps should enable you to do this:

- **Set 'work time' limits** – decide on what is work time and what is not and set a clear divide. You can use features on devices and apps to set 'quiet time', when notifications will not appear and you will not be alerted by them. Do not be afraid to switch devices and data connections off, such as wireless Internet. If you feel that you are using digital technologies too much, you could set yourself 'usage limits' where you limit your screen time.

- **Organise, de-clutter and simplify** – choose digital tools with settings and features which decrease information overload. You can do this by turning 'pushed' notifications, messages and content off in the settings. To organise and de-clutter your digital workspace, create folders for different types of content and start to organise what you receive and how you receive it. A good example of this is in Google's Gmail and Microsoft's Outlook, which enable you to create thematic folders for new emails to go into. This stops new emails from filling up your inbox in a disorganised fashion. Social networks, such as Twitter, Google +, LinkedIn and Facebook have features which allow you to organise the people and organisations you follow into lists, circles and groups, which is helpful for organising the flow of social information. Finally, you may want to consider using tools which automate the connection and syncing of data. Tools such as If This Then That allow you to make your productivity apps talk to each other and carry out tasks in the background. This can include creating a digital note for you into note-taking software, such as Evernote every time someone tweets on a particular topic, or emailing you the content of the tweet. You could also sync up your various social network and media accounts with the contacts in your smartphone (this can usually be done through the contacts settings), so that all available information on your contacts is automatically updated when they change them.

- **Decide on multiple or single devices** – if you have a multiple devices, you should consider making one for leisure/personal use only and the other for work only. Not only will this add an extra level of security to work accounts, but will also help you to keep separate digital environments for work and leisure time.

- **Work out what you need from a productivity tool and choose one** – there are lots of apps and services out there which claim to be the best at a particular task, but really one is all you need. Choosing one app for your calendar/ tasks, one cloud storage and one email account for all your work tasks can reduce the complexity involved and allow you to make best use of your time. The apps you choose should meet your need for privacy, safety and security, should be easy to navigate, and offer useful features, rather than add-ons you will not use.

Example

Adam is a teacher and assessor at a local college. He teaches business and retail, but spends most of the time visiting and assessing a large number of apprentices in the area. It is the evening and he is at home making dinner, his tablet PC is next to him and he is following a recipe from an app. Other apps, such as email and social networks are running in the background and occasionally the tablet will buzz to indicate that a new messages and updates have been received. He feels relaxed. He finishes cooking and sits down to eat. He puts on music on his tablet PC. The music is interrupted three times by a noise to indicating that new emails have been received to his work email account. He breaks from eating to read the emails. They are from his students, clarifying an assignment task he has set. He feels obliged to answer them immediately and breaks from eating. He spends the rest of the evening working at his tablet PC.

Think about Adam's situation and advise him on the following:

- *Developing a better work–life balance.*

- *Making digital tools work for him, instead of letting them dictate how and when he works.*

Selecting tools for learning and teaching

There are two main reasons why we may want to use digital tools for learning and in our teaching:

- Designing activities, learning resources and learning content with, and delivering them through, digital tools.

- Teaching students how to use digital tools and enabling them to create with them.

Both of these purposes require the teacher to:

- Have pedagogical reasoning for using them.

- Plan thoroughly the design and delivery.

- Acquire knowledge and skills in the digital tools.

When planning and forming pedagogical reasoning for your use of digital tools you should first consider the different types of digital tools available, listed earlier in this chapter in the 'What are digital tools?' section and the evaluation and selection criteria mentioned in the previous two sections. In addition to these, you should also consider the following criteria (some of which will be more relevant to specific situations than others):

- **Will it be beneficial to my learners** – what will be the advantages and disadvantages of using a digital tool? What affect will it have on their engagement? What outcomes does it satisfy? Will it add to their existing skills and will they be able to transfer the skills?

- **Will it aid/improve teaching** – does it make it easier to deliver the topic/subject? Does it meet/exceed the learning outcomes? What benefits does it have (e.g. can multimedia, such as video, audio, image, animation and text be connected together for ease of delivery)? Is it assessable?

- **Check the accessibility** – where you require students to use digital tools and interact with digital content, check that they are able to accessible to them, considering their needs. Jisc Digital Media (no date) have a guide to checking the accessibility of digital content and Mozilla Webmaker (no date) have a guide to accessible Web design. In general, you should consider the following criteria:

o   Check that fonts are sans serif and the size is changeable.

o   Check that screen reading software will be able to read the website aloud and is able to give context to images (this is done through the use of alt-text. When you hover over an image, alt-text is displayed, giving the title and or context of the image). If you are creating the resource, check in the help guide of the software how to create alt-text.

o   Check that background colours are changeable. This is particularly helpful to students with dyslexia and colour-sensitivities.

- **Check for appropriateness** – if you are using third-party content and tools, check that the content is right for your students and your curriculum. Consider:

o   Is the level right? The content may be have been made for learners at a higher or lower level to yours. If it is wrong, can you adapt it?

o   Is the age right? Video content especially can sometimes contain nasty surprises such as abusive language, violence and sexual references which may be inappropriate or offensive.

o   Is the content right? Think about the information, facts and figures being presented: are they referenced? Is the information context or location specific, and suitable to your curriculum?

- **Check the quality** – if the content or tool is of poor design quality it may not work properly, or may be overly-complicated. The structure of the content or tool should be clear and straightforward. If the quality is poor, then this could act as a barrier and exclude learners.

When you are ready to start designing learning and teaching digital tools and content, take a look at the pedagogy and 'Spotlight on…' sections in the previous chapter for ideas of methods you could use.

Activity

To get an idea of how others have designed and used digital tools and content for learning and teaching purposes, search the Jorum database. The 'Further education' page (Jorum, 2015) is full of content and resources on a wide variety of FE subjects and topics.

Creativity

We each have particular talents and skills. These may be artistic talents and design skills, a flair for creating engaging activities and learning resources, or an ability to turn subject knowledge and theory into accessible learning suitable for particular groups. As teachers our practice allows us to gain, apply and refine these talents and skills as we encourage our learners to discover and develop their own. With the wide variety of digital technologies now available to teachers, we are more able than ever to channel our talents and skills into creating rich digital content. The benefits of doing this include:

- Engaging learners with new learning resources and content.

- Developing new skills in manipulating and creating digital content.

- Improving your confidence with digital technologies.

- Better understanding of digital technologies, which could have a series of positive knock-on effects.

Talent and skills can only thrive with the right culture, environment and access to training and resources. These conditions alone will not guarantee creativity and innovation, though – we also each need to be positively engaged in the process; doing it for the right reasons, and building our confidence and skills at the right pace for us.

Carlile and Jordan (2012) asserted that the revolution in digital technologies has 'democratised creativity', by giving everyone the freedom to create and publish, but freedom is different from enablement and many people choose to mainly consume and rarely produce (see Chapter 3 for the definitions of these activities). This is exemplified by the 'one per cent rule' of digital participation (Horowitz, 2006) which is used as a 'rule of thumb' guide to how many people will participate digitally, based on the type of interaction (Johnson, 2012). Not taken too literally, the rule says that the majority of people will simply 'consume' a digital medium, while a few will 'synthesise' or actively engage with it, and as few as one per cent will be the 'creators' who edit, create/produce and add content to it (Horowitz, 2006). To improve your digital skills, learn new knowledge and improve your Web presence requires gaining the confidence to 'be the one per cent', and letting your creativity flow.

Activity

Think about each of these and the digital skills needed to do them: video creation, editing and sharing; app/software design; website design; blog writing; learning object design and creation.

- *Which would you like to learn and how would it be beneficial to your development?*

- *In what ways would having these skills improve your learning, teaching and development?*

- *Conduct a search to find information on how to learn these skills, as well as free beginners software. You could try searching on a Web search engine, an app marketplace/store, or in a specific search tool, social media site or other database. Use the evaluation criteria in Chapter 7 to help you filter through what you find.*

- *Use the Mozilla Webmaker website (https://webmaker.org/en-US/resources) as a starting point to identify sources of learning of these skills.*

To make creativity happen requires a mix of the following ingredients:

- Ideas and plans.

- Imagination and enthusiasm.

- Time and space (both physical and mental).

- Reasons and expected outcomes.

To then start using digital tools to express this creativity requires the following conditions in your workplace:

- **Creative culture** – are you encouraged to be creative? Are you allowed to express your ideas, given the space to develop them and put them into practice?

- **Experimentation space** – are you allowed to explore new methods and approaches and try them out? Are there consequences if it doesn't work, or are you given the space to reflect on the experience and learn where it went wrong?

- **Sharing and collaborative culture** – are you given the forums to express opinions, discover new ideas, share good practice and build collaborative working relationships?

Many teachers would say that they are not given the conditions above at work, with the most common reason being given that there is not enough time to do these things. However, it could be argued that we find ourselves in the perfect creative spaces every day – the classroom and our lesson planning time. In these spaces, we experience planning, designing, making, building, learning, knowledge transfer, the sharing of ideas and skills. All delivered through the mediums we choose. Therefore the classroom is the perfect place to start experimenting with digital tools and creating new content that you can eventually share online.

In Chapter 7 we will look at how you can showcase your talents and skills online in order to build a digital profile, and Chapter 9 looks at licensing models for the digital content you create.

Summary

In this chapter you have learned:

- What is meant by the term 'digital tools'.

- How to approach the selection of digital tools for professional purposes.

- How to select and use digital tools to be a more productive professional.

- How to select and use digital tools to design and deliver learning and teaching.

- About your own usage of digital tools and their relationship with your creative talents.

References and further reading

Berners-Lee, T (1999) *Weaving the Web: The Origins and Future of the World Wide Web by its Inventor*. London: Orion Business.

Brabazon, T (2013) *Digital Dieting: From Information Obesity to Intellectual Fitness*. Aldershot: Ashgate.

Carlile, O and Jordan, A (2012) *Approaches to Creativity: A Guide for Teachers*. Maidenhead: Open University Press.

Goodyear, P and Carvalho, L (2013) 'The analysis of complex learning environments', in H Beetham and R Sharpe (eds) *Rethinking Pedagogy for a Digital Age: Designing for 21st Century Learning*. 2nd edn. Abingdon: Routledge. pp. 49–63.

Horowitz, B (2006) 'Creators, synthesizers, and consumers', in Elatable blog, 16 February. Available at: http://blog.elatable.com/2006/02/creators-synthesizers-and-consumers.html.

Hyperakt and Vizzuality (2012) *The Evolution of the Web*. Available at: http://www.evolutionoftheweb.com/.

Jisc Digital Media (no date) *Basic Guide to Accessibility*. Available at: http://www.jiscdigitalmedia.ac.uk/guide/basic-guide-to-accessibility.

Johnson, B (2012) 'Is the 1% rule dead? The BBC thinks so, but it's wrong', in Gigaom Research blog, 6 May. Available at: https://gigaom.com/2012/05/06/bbc-1-percent-rule/.

Jorum (2015) *Jorum Further Education Collection*. Available at: http://www.jorum.ac.uk/#jorum-further-education.

Mozilla Webmaker (no date) *Design and Accessibility: Creating Universally Effective Communications through Web Resources*. Available at: https://webmaker.org/en-US/resources/literacy/weblit-DesignAccessibility.

O'Reilly, T (2005) 'What is Web 2.0? Design patterns and business models for the next generation of software', O'Reilly blog, 30 September. Available at: http://oreilly.com/pub/a/web2/archive/what-is-web-20.html?page=3.

Pearson, C and Hussain, Z (2015) 'Smartphone use, addiction, narcissism, and personality: a mixed methods investigation', *International Journal of Cyber Behaviour, Psychology and Learning*, 5(1): 17–32. DOI: 10.4018/ijcbpl.2015010102.

In this chapter you will learn:

- To consider your needs for digital information and media and start to think strategically.
- About definitions and frameworks of information literacy and how to apply them to your practice in the FE and Skills sector.
- About the different types of digital information and media available and the factors to consider when using them.
- To understand search processes and apply a suitable approach to your own practice.
- To appreciate the factors which affect our evaluation of resources in the digital age.
- How to organise your digital information and media resources and sources.

Links to the Digitally Literate FE and Skills Teacher Framework

4.   Develops a critical approach to digital information and media while becoming more information literate.

The Web provides us with a wealth of information and media in an ever-expanding variety of formats. Very often though, we only require a small amount of it for the tasks we need to complete. Knowing which sources to search and which resources to use requires consideration of many factors, such as the task in hand and how quality can be assessed. In the context of learning and teaching it is vitally important that we understand these factors and make good decisions. This chapter considers how we can develop our knowledge and understanding of digital information and media and apply processes and strategies to our practice.

What are your needs for digital information and media?

Broadly, when we think about our practice as teachers we can group why we need information and media and how we use it into the following categories:

- **As learners of teacher education and our subject disciplines** we use digital information and media to gain new knowledge, to understand ideas and theories, and to find evidence to support our approach. This includes learning about pedagogical approaches and the thorough knowledge we need of our subject area.

- **As practitioners and professionals** we use digital information and media to further our understanding of our subject and curriculum areas, to discover new ideas and approaches and to better understand our roles and responsibilities. This includes undertaking formal and non-formal professional development activities.

- **As teachers planning and delivering learning** we understand that the abilities to learn and work independently, to find and reuse information and media, and to be critical of it, are important life skills all learners need to develop. We use our knowledge, understanding and appreciation of the research process and subject-specific information sources to teach learners the value of good research skills and evaluative approaches to using information.

For each one of these categories, the types of information resources required and the source of them may be different. However, the strategy you use and the process you work through will probably be broadly similar. As you work through this chapter consider the process you go through when finding and using digital information and media for the purposes above. By understanding and keeping in mind the initial need for information and media, the approach you take and the strategy you develop will be more focused and reflective of these needs.

Example

Phil has worked as an electrical engineering lecturer for the last five years, and worked within the industry for many years before that. As a subject specialist he feels he is knowledgeable about his subject and has a wealth of experience. He regularly keeps his subject knowledge up to date by reading updates and using other resources from the website of the Institute of Engineering and Technology's (IET), as well as from a couple of trade websites. While undertaking a teacher training qualification he has to search for information in new locations, such as library databases and within Web-based sources he has not used before. He is also recommended to access various digital groups and communities through social media and to watch and listen to digital media from a variety of locations.

As he learns more about the different types of digital information and media sources available and uses them more and more, Phil realises that he needs to adapt his approach to finding subject-based information and media. Later, Phil is chatting to the Learning Resources Manager about how much he has learned and how he would like to find a way to engage the learners on his level 3 and level 4 programmes with accessing and using different information and media types. Together they plan a session on being more critical and discerning about which digital sources to use, as well getting the learners to access much better Web resources for their subject. Phil finds that learning about digital information and media is not only helping the learners to develop their subject knowledge, but also allowing himself to learn in new ways.

Developing a strategy and becoming information literate

As we use the Web, we each develop our own approach to searching for, evaluating, using and managing digital information and media. In developing our digital literacy skills, we must each learn to deeply understand this process and become more critical and strategic in our approach to it. In doing so, we become more aware of and knowledgeable about the variety of resources that exist and develop a better understanding of how to choose between them, find, identify and evaluate, analyse and assess them. By developing your critical and strategic use of information you will become more information literate, and can apply this to all aspects of your practice.

The skills of information literacy and applications to the FE and Skills sector

As with digital literacy, many definitions of information literacy, and agendas for its development, are put forward by a range of organisations and bodies. This includes the United Nations Educational, Scientific and Cultural Organization's *Alexandria Proclamation on Information Literacy and definition* (UNESCO, 2005), the Jisc 'i-Skills' project (Jisc, 2005) and Education Scotland's (2014) *Information and Critical Literacy* initiative and the *National Information Literacy Framework for Scotland* (Irving and Crawford, 2009). The definition of information literacy that is most widely accepted in the UK is the one put forward by The Chartered Institute of Library and Information Professionals (CILIP). They define information literacy as:

> *knowing when and why you need information, where to find it, and how to evaluate, use and communicate it in an ethical manner.*

> (CILIP, 2004)

This definition allows us to step back and ask a set of critical questions about our understanding of digital information and media and the research process needed to find and use them. We might ask the following questions throughout the process:

- **Why do I need information from another source?** For example, is it to learn something new? Add to my understanding? Improve my awareness and knowledge? To answer a question? To back something up with facts? To develop my arguments?

- **What type(s) of information do I need for this task?** For example, statistics? Opinion? Definitions/an overview? Examples/case studies? Research/project findings? Visual or audio evidence/representation?

- **Are there any digital sources I can go straight to for this information/media or which search tools will I use to find this information/media?** For example, where will I search? How will I search? What keywords will I use? How will I refine and focus my search?

- **How will I evaluate the results I find and make decisions on if and how to use them?** For example, how will I judge the credibility of a resource? How can I tell if it is current and accurate? Is it factual and evidence based? Are the publisher and author credible?

- **How will I use the information I find and organise it?** For example, will I quote from it? Paraphrase it? Apply it to another context? Share it? Comment on it or review it? Annotate it? Will I use it as I find it, or store it for later use?

- **How does ethical usage apply to how I am using it?** For example, is referencing enough? Can I reuse it for free? Is there a licence attached to the content? Do I need to be careful in how I share and use this content? (There is more on using digital content ethically and legally in Chapter 9.)

The *Seven Pillars of Information Literacy* by the Society of College, National and University Libraries (SCONUL, 2011) presents the questions above as the following seven 'pillars', or steps, of the information and media research process:

- Identify

- Scope

- Plan

- Gather

- Evaluate

- Manage

- Present.

Although designed with higher education in mind, the Seven Pillars model provides good explanations of what is required to become literate in each pillar and most of the content can be directly applied to learning and teaching throughout the FE and Skills sector.

Activity

Think about the types of assignments you set learners which involve searching for, finding and using information and consider the questions below:

- *How much guidance do you provide on the processes involved in this kind of activity?*

- *Do you have clear expectations on where learners will look for information, what they will search for, how they will evaluate what they find, how they will analyse the information and how they will present it to you?*

- *Are these expectations built into assessment criteria and learning outcomes?*

- *Do you believe that learners need guidance in these processes?*

- *How can your learners be engaged effectively in understanding and developing their information literacy?*

In the FE and Skills sector parts of information literacy are often taught as part of a wider approach to study skills or functional skills, or are embedded into the curriculum through information research tasks and assignments. Over the years, they have some-times been referred to as 'information skills' or 'information-gathering and retrieval skills'. Teachers in the FE and Skills sector very rarely frame information literacy as a distinct set of skills and very often learners are not made aware of the importance of developing a 'start-to-finish' process or strategy. The metacognitive approach (as described in Chapter 10) is particularly useful when applied to this context though, as understanding that you are learning a strategy for finding and using digital information and media allows learners to take responsibility for the process and understand the importance of critical thinking.

Despite the obvious benefits to all teachers and learners, many still see information literacy as 'too academic' for the FE and Skills sector. This is often not helped by the academic language used in models and skill sets and the focus upon higher education within them.

Information literacy is relevant to all learners and teachers across the FE and Skills sector though. As all the other strands of digital literacy, being information literate is key to our development as informed, critical thinking and creative digital citizens, as well as becoming independent lifelong learners. Hind and Moss (2011: 233) categorise information literacy as a 'highly transferable' employability skill which can be utilised in a wide range of real-life scenarios, such as researching company information before applying for a job or researching product information before buying a product. UNESCO's (2005) *Alexandria Proclamation on Information Literacy* lists information literacy as a 'basic human right in a digital world', which seems appropriate, as without it digital information and media relevant to our lives, our social interactions, our access to public services, our access to lifelong learning opportunities and our job/career prospects, are all severely reduced.

As with all the other strands of digital literacy, it is not until we put information literacy into context that its value to our lives, learning and work becomes apparent. Regardless of our industry, sector or subject area there is a relevance for information literacy.

Activity

Consider where information literacy fits within the curricula/programmes you teach.

- *Is it more relevant to some than others?*

- *Do you already teach it (you may or may not refer to it as information literacy)?*

- *Is this an area where collaborative practice could improve the experience for both you and your learners?*

- *If you have librarians/learning resources staff within your institution speak to them about how they can help with the learning and teaching of information literacy.*

When considering how to embed and integrate information literacy into your curriculum it is a good idea to take a holistic approach, looking at where the skills fit and putting them in to context. *A New Curriculum for Information Literacy* (ANCIL) (Secker and Coonan, 2011) provides a framework and audit tool which allows teachers to look at their subject and curriculum area in order to integrate information literacy appropriately.

It is also important to consider the language you will use to describe information literacy to your learners. At the University of Derby, we have recently used the simple mantra 'Think, Search, Find' to promote library search tools and this is a neat summary of information literacy.

The rest of this chapter focuses on the following elements of finding and using digital information and media:

- Understanding

- Searching and filtering

- Evaluation

- Organisation and storage.

Understanding and identifying digital information and media types

The terms 'resource' and 'source' are used throughout this chapter. These are the definitions of the two terms so as to disambiguate them:

- **Resource** – this is used to refer to the individual item of information or media. Examples of resources include articles, posts, comments, documents, Web pages, data sets, video clips, audio clips and images. Resources will always be found within a source.

- **Source** – this is used to refer to three linked, but sometimes different, identifiers of the resource's origin:

  o The place you found the resource – its location.

  o The publisher of the resource.

  o The author/creator of the resource.

Digital information and media resources may be found in a variety of places, such as a website, a blog, a Facebook group, page or profile, a YouTube profile or a forum/community. These resources may have been published by the author of the material, or re-published by a different person. The author may either be an individual or an organisation.

Search engines, such as Google, Bing and Yahoo!, search across both sources and resources to find content (although they cannot access everything), but do not distinguish between the two in search results. Therefore, many learners believe that the search engine is the source of their information, when in fact it is a medium through which to find both sources and resources.

The Web contains a wide variety of different sources and resources of digital information and media, and this variety continues to evolve and diversify. The evolution of the Web into Web 2.0 (see Chapter 5 for details) has allowed for this diversity and therefore digital information and media now come in many forms:

- **'Traditional' websites** – these are the types of digital information we have been used to since the start of the Web. A collection of webpages which form a website. Most organisations, companies, media outlets and many individuals have a website. Most make use now of some of the features listed below.

- **Social media and networks** – blogs, forums, wikis, networks such as Facebook, Twitter and LinkedIn, audio and video sharing such as YouTube, websites inviting partici-pation. These are sources which invite all users to create and add content, edit content and share content. The information and media within them is user generated. Anyone can be an author, creator and publisher of content.

- **Open and licensed resources** – including open access (OA) articles and books, open educational resources (OERs) and open government-licensed (OGL) publications and creative commons (CC) licensed materials. These are resources which are free at the point of use, but have a specific licence attached on how they can be used, and/or have gone through quality processes before publication on the Web. Very often OER resources are found in networks aimed solely at professionals within a field (e.g. teachers), or in the case of OGL publications are available from an official website. CC licences can be used by the owner of any digital content. OA publications are a method for facilitating repu-table and scholarly publishing to continue in the digital age, but the author or publisher incurs the costs, making the resources free at the point of use. These resources can take the form of articles, e-books, reports, documents, presentations and learning objects (as discussed in the last chapter). Most of these resources are designed to be downloaded and may require additional software to open and make use of them – for example, a PDF viewer, word processor or presentation software, all of which are available as a range of free and paid-for software available for all operating systems and devices. The next chapter looks at how you can work with these types of resources to boost your digital identity, and Chapter 9 explores digital licensing more.

- **Premium resources** – these are resources which require payment for use or down-load. This can include e-books, digital music and video files and subscription journal articles. Usually they are provided in a format which limits reuse and manipulation, but the software needed to use them is usually available in both free and paid-for versions, such e-book and PDF viewers, MP3 and digital media players. Sometimes publishers of these resources make use of digital rights management (DRM) software, which limits the amount of times a resource can be used or the number of devices it can be used on, and some files can only be used with specific software and apps – for example, Amazon Kindle e-books.

The differences between these sources and resources can sometimes be subtle and it is not always immediately obvious what type is on the screen in front of you. Getting used to identifying the types is beneficial though, as it allows us to ask critical questions about accuracy, reliability and credibility.

Activity

Look at the descriptions above and think about the different types of digital information and media sources you search or browse through on a regular basis for work purposes.

- *What types of resources are you finding and using and what sort of information is contained within them?*
- *Is the information always suitable for your needs?*
- *Is it based upon research findings and/or backed up with evidence, or is it more opinion based?*
- *How can you find and use more quality sources and resources?*

Premium vs. free resources

The debate over the quality of freely available resources when compared with traditionally published resources has raged since the dawn of the Web and will probably continue to be debated for many years to come. Within education, this is a controversial topic with some teachers and assessors preferring to see traditional resources dominating references lists, while others prefer a mix of traditional and non-traditional. There is also a difference in attitudes depending upon the subject.

The majority of this controversy has arisen since Wikipedia launched in 2001 with the slogan 'The free encyclopedia that anyone can edit' (Wikipedia, 2014). This digital encyclopaedia, as well as other sources like it, started a revolution of Web publishing that everyone could participate in. As Hague and Payton (2010) of FutureLab point out 'Creating and editing information is no longer the preserve of the educated elite; knowledge and information… can be created and edited by anyone'. The problem that has arisen from this revolution has been one of credibility, as suddenly subject information is being authored, edited and published by persons unknown and is extremely easy to find and access through search engines. Many teachers have spent many years trying to stop learners from using Wikipedia for this very reason, but in recent years Wikipedia has become but one of many sources of user-generated information on the Web and many in education have come to see the value of it in the research process. Very often though, this translates into the advice that learners should 'never copy or quote from Wikipedia' and 'never include Wikipedia in your references list'. David White (2014) of the Jisc-funded Digital Visitors and Residents project (Jisc, 2011) argues that this is a dangerous way to approach learning about using information, as it could create 'a learning black market' where learners do one thing in reality in order to learn, but report another to their teacher. Researchers on Project Information Literacy at the University of Washington have found that Wikipedia and other easily accessible and free Web-based information sources are the starting point for most learners when conducting research. The learners they surveyed saw Wikipedia as a good way to get started before moving on to more traditional resources (Head and Eisenberg, 2010). They make the point that not recognising this as a valid part of the research process will only serve to widen the gap between education and the practice of individuals.

For the FE and Skills sector in particular, there needs to be a strong connection between knowledge and skills learned and real-world practice. Therefore, the more suitable approach is to recognise these resources as being part of the initial stages of research and developing an approach to teaching good practice. For example, Wikipedia can be a really useful source of information when wanting to gain an overview of a topic, and finding definitions and the references list can lead on to other good resources where more in-depth knowledge can be gained. Head and Eisenberg (2010) refer to this process as 'presearching'.

Example

Mo has noticed that his learners use the first few search results and Wikipedia to get an overview of topics when starting assignments. Instead of criticising this approach he decides to embrace it and turn it into an activity. He designs a task where learners search for and evaluate free dictionaries and encyclopaedias available online and create a list that the class agrees are useful for everyone to use in the presearching phase. The learners engage immediately and show themselves to be quite adept at judging the suitability of the sources. Mo also notices that some of them gain in confidence through the exercise. By the end of the session the class have decided on a set of presearch sources they will use to search for definitions and to get an overview. Mo decides that he will include a 'presearch references list' in addition to the main list in the next assignment brief so they can gain credit for their approach.

Activity

Search for 'free dictionary' and 'free encyclopaedia' in a search engine and look at the results.

- *Which of the many free-to-use dictionaries and encyclopaedias would you prefer your learners to use?*
- *How could you engage your learners in judging the value of each?*

Searching and filtering

The way in which the Web has evolved and the amount of digital content it provides encourage us to become detached from the search and discovery process and uncritical of our approach. Popular wisdom dictates that typing a few words into a search engine and clicking the top result will generally provide you with the information or media you need. However, we know as teachers that for many purposes, including learning and studying, this is not enough and deeper thinking is needed in order to find and use good-quality content. It is also important to recognise that good search skills are needed throughout life and that not taking care when searching can lead to finding bogus, inaccurate or misleading information which could cause a variety of problems.

An interesting example of this was presented on the BBC's consumer rights programme, *Watchdog*, in 2009: the programme featured a story on members of the public who had been scammed by a service offering information and advice on child benefit through a pre-mium rate phone number. Those caught out had typed 'child benefit' into the search engine, Google. What appeared to be the top result displayed a premium rate phone number for an advice line, which many had called, only to be given very little useful information and to be charged £31.50 for the call duration. The information, advice and forms they needed were actually freely available online through UK government's portal Gov.uk, but, even though this was the top search result, it did not appear at the top because the owner of the premium rate phone line had taken out an advert which appeared at the top of the search results (details of the programme can be found here: 'Tony', 2009). Very often people are unaware of how search results are structured, with paid-for advertisements in a panel, sometimes above or to the side of the actual results, and increasingly, results from other products by the search provider given prominence.

What is required is a critical approach to the search process that includes thought-out steps which allows for key questions to be considered at different points. This can be achieved by developing a search strategy which includes a resource understanding stage, a presearch stage, a keyword/search terms development stage and an evaluation and analysis stage.

When undertaking a search for information and media, the keywords and search terms you select are critical to what results you will get back. Search engines are becoming better at understanding 'natural language', that is understanding the context and semantics of the information you require, and this is why, in recent times, searching for a question such as 'how long does it take to travel from Macclesfield to London?' will provide driving direc-tions and routes and direct links to that specific journey in train operators' ticket-booking websites. As a result many learners approach researching for information for assignments in the same way and get back inconsistent results. Many search tools within websites and library databases do not understand natural language searching and therefore a more tra-ditional approach to generating keywords and using a toolkit of search tips and tricks is required. These work across all search tools, academic databases and search engines.

The search tool kit

- **Mindmap** – pick out the synonyms, acronyms and related terms/concepts and lay them all out in a mindmap. As you search you can pick out terms to try and, as you discover more, you can make a note of them in your mindmap. A wide range of mindmapping software and apps is available.

- **Speech marks** – the addition of speech marks to two words or more allows the search tool to recognise them as a phrase, which leads to more accurate search results – e.g. 'sports coaching'.

- **Boolean operators** – these allow for search terms to be connected together or disambiguated from each other.

o Adding AND between two search terms ensures that both terms are found within one resource. For example, searching Sports AND Coaching would find resources containing both words, but not necessarily together.

o Adding OR between two search terms allows for resources containing alternative words to be found. For example, searching Football OR Soccer would find resources on both and would increase the amount of results.

o Adding NOT between two search terms can potentially reduce the number of results you receive and focus in the resources you actually want. For example, searching Football NOT Soccer is likely to bring up results which exclude many articles from the USA.

- **Wildcards** – the wildcard is the question mark symbol and can be placed within a word where there are multiple or alternative spellings. For example, the word *behaviour* does not have a 'u' in the American English spelling. Replacing the 'u' with a wildcard (*behavio?r*) would find resources with either spelling.

- **Truncation** – the truncation is the asterisk symbol and this is used where there are many possible endings to the root of a word. Adding the symbol will return results with all possible endings. For example, searching behaviour* will find resources containing behaviour, behaviours, behavioural and behaviourism.

- **Filters** – very often we search and then, upon studying the results, realise that something was missing from or search, or that it is not focused enough. We could run the search again, but very often databases and search tools have filters that allow you to change the results based upon factors such as the following: date created, geography and location it is applicable to, language of the resource and availability for instant download.

Activity

Conducting a search for professional literature on a subject.

- *Think about a topic you are interested in professionally (this could either be related to teaching practice or your subject specialism) and produce a mindmap of the synonyms, acronyms and related terms/concepts.*

- *Search an **academic database** (these provide the details and abstracts to journal articles and professional reports, and link to the full text of the document where it is freely available and where your institution pays for access – ask your learning resource centre/library what they provide access to) or Google Scholar (this is a freely accessible academic database, but it can only provide access to what is freely available online).*

Evaluation

As the example from *Watchdog* above shows, being able to evaluate sources of information is key to being critical and informed when searching for information and media.

When evaluating information and media resources, we generally look for the following indicators in order to judge credibility, accuracy, currency and usefulness to our needs:

- **Author** – this could be a person or an organisation. What are the author's credentials? Are they an expert/professional in the field? What qualifies them to provide credible information on the subject? Are they affiliated with any particular organisations/businesses, movements or theories which could affect their objectivity?

- **Date** – is the information current and up to date? Does this matter for this type of information?

- **Location/audience** – where was the information published and at whom is it aimed? Is the information country specific or would it be relevant to/true of any country?

- **Language and voice** – is the language and style formal or informal? Is it written to inform, entertain, instruct, publicise or sell? Does it use good spelling and grammar, which could indicate editorial control? Is evidence used to support claims, or is it based upon opinion?

- **Publisher and publication** – if it is formally published the publisher should be clear. Look for the producer/owner/editor of the website. This might be found in the 'About Us' or 'Contact Us' section. Is the author the same as the publisher? If so, then what process of review has taken place before it was published? In what format is the information published and to what standard and quality?

- **URL** – if the resource is Web based, what can we tell from URL? Does it indicate where the website is located (e.g. co.uk would indicate a UK-based site)? Does it have a suffix which is restricted to certain types of organisations (e.g. only UK government departments and institutions are able to hold a .gov.uk suffix and only UK-based publicly funded further and higher education establishments are able to hold a .ac.uk suffix).

- **References** – does the resource contain referencing and does it use this to cite other sources and support its claims?

With such a wide and diverse range of digital information and media available from an infinite number of sources, the need to critically evaluate is more important than ever before. An increasingly vast array of social networks/media, apps, websites and digital tools contains the information we need and use, and this means that we have to look closely at individual sources and resources to identify the location of some of the indicators above. The author/creator details are, for example, given in different places depending upon the source and sometimes it is difficult to decide which piece of information relates to the author's details/profile. The following examples demonstrate how this can vary between different sources:

- **A Tweet from a Twitter user** – author's name, credentials, affiliations and links to other profiles/website may or may not be given. You may have to judge credibility and quality by comparing the Tweet against others the person has Tweeted or by looking at whom they follow and who follows them. The content of the Tweet you want to use might be quoted or re-purposed (re-Tweeted) from another Tweeter.

- **A video on social media** (such as YouTube or Vimeo) – the profile of the uploader will be available to view, but this may not be the same person or organisation who produced the video. Looking for an 'official' upload of the video is more likely to indicate the currency, give context and background to the video and provide links to official websites and other resources.

- **A non-fiction e-book on a subject** – these can be formally published or self-published. If self-published, we need to establish who the author is and their credentials and if editorial or peer review has taken place. This process would help to establish authenticity, accuracy and quality. Reviews of the e-books could be used to see how others rate it and its contents, but questions about the author of the review would also need to be asked.

The complexity and varying nature of digital sources and resources means that the locations of source details cannot be standardised. With more traditional forms of published information, such as books, magazines and journals, details such as author, title, date and publisher are listed in standard places, such as on the front cover or on a bibliographical information page. However, with digital information and media increasingly taking the form of user-generated 'posts' (e.g. Tweets, blog posts, comments, reviews and uploads), there is a blurring of the source details and the content. The following features are common to these resources and could be used to evaluate them:

- **Username/handle** – this identifies the individual posting the information. It could take the form of the person's actual name (as with Facebook), or could take the form of an alias (as with Twitter and YouTube). Some sources, such as blogs, forums and review websites may allow users to use a mixture.

- **Profile** – this gives details about the individual. Usually clicking the user's username/handle will take you to their profile page. The amount of information displayed will depend upon how much the user has inputted, although some services require a minimum amount of information. Details of jobs and career experience, expertise and skills, and affiliations or links to organisations and other individuals are likely to be useful. Links to other profiles on professional networks (such as LinkedIn or Academic.edu) or a link to a profile page on an organisation's website could be useful.

- **Date and timestamp** – this could be used to assess currency, but may be of limited use depending on the type of information. If it is a longer publication, such as a full blog post or an e-book the date may be of more use.

- **The social network/media or service/publication provider** – this can tell you a lot about the credibility/validity of the information. Question why the information has been published in a particular place and whether this makes a difference to its reliability. A detailed blog post from a verifiable and respected author can be as useful as a published journal article, but this may have been to avoid scrutiny and process.

- **Friends and followers** – it can be really useful to look at a list of whom the person is following, as well as who is following them. Does their friends and followers list tell you anything about the following: are they linked to other valued professionals? Do they have regular interactions with these professionals? Are they respected and trusted as a knowledgeable person in their field?

- **Posts, likes, scores, reviews, comments** – when assessing the credibility of a group, forum or organisation it may be useful to analyse some of the content/discussion going on. Is it well written? How much bias is evident? Is it informed comment or uninformed opinion? Is it moderate and fair, or extreme in nature? If assessing the credibility of an individual, you can ask the same questions of their posts, likes, scores, reviews and/or comments. You can also look at the nature of their output and ask if it is mostly related to their professional area, mostly unrelated and unprofessional, or a mixture of the two. Does the balance seem appropriate? White (2014) has observed that learners do pay close attention to these factors and actively use them to judge quality and credibility.

- **Influence** – does the person posting the information appear to have social influence? You can look at the number of views their posts achieve, and at the number of replies, comments and shares they receive. However, you still need to keep the ideas of professional quality, balance and evidence in mind in order to judge the overall quality.

Of course no individual metric listed above will give an overall answer on the credibility of a resource and it is important to develop your critical judgement based upon a combination of the metrics. Look out for elements which stand out as being inconsistent, out of place and inappropriate, as these may trigger critical questions based upon the indicators.

Activity

Search for 'learning theories' in a search engine.

- *Looking at the top five results, evaluate each based upon the criteria discussed in this section.*

- *Which appears to be the most trustworthy and which appears to be the least?*

- *Which would you use (if any) when learning about this subject for a teaching qualification or for professional development?*

Organising your sources and resources

Organisation skills are something we each either have or wish we had. When it comes to organising and managing our sources and resources a plethora of digital solutions exists which can make the task much easier. There are various types of solutions available, but most claim to do at least one of the following, with some doing more than one:

- **Bookmarking** – these are tools that allow you to collect data (such as URLs and the title) of Web-based content (such as web pages, online documents and media content) and save them locally so that you can view them later. You can organise these links alphabetically into folders and sometimes with keywords, for easy access later. All Web browsers on your devices, such as Microsoft's Internet Explorer, have this functionality. Some browsers, such as Google's Chrome, allow you to create an account and sync your bookmarks to the browsers on your different devices.

- **Social bookmarking** – this has all the features of bookmarking, except the bookmarks are not stored locally on your device. It is instead a Web-based (or cloud-based) storage service for your bookmarks that you can choose to share with a world-wide community of users. Conversely, you can also access the bookmarks of others. Many users create subject-themed folders of bookmarks that become popular with the people who follow their collections. Examples of social bookmarking services include Diigo and Delicious. Diigo also gives you additional tools that allow you to highlight and annotate documents. Social bookmarking is a key element of social networks, such as Facebook, Twitter and LinkedIn, where we share links to resources we find online and some have facilities to store and organise content we discover. Twitter provides two useful tools for storing and organising content: the 'favourite' button allows us to store individual tweets into our own favourites area and 'lists' allows us to create folders on topics we are interested in and add relevant Twitter accounts to it, in order to see a customised feed on that particular topic. My own Twitter Lists can be viewed and subscribed to here: http://twitter.com/jonwhite82/lists.

- **Cloud-based file storage** – this can be split into two types:

  o Cloud storage solutions, such as Dropbox and Google Drive, which allow you to securely upload and save your files (documents and media content) to a folder on the service's servers, allowing you to access, download and upload from all of your devices, while keeping the documents private to you and those you individually choose to share files with. This would be useful in terms of organising your sources, for when you download documents (such as journal articles and reports) and need flexible storage.

  o Social bookmarking networks with file storage, such as Mendeley, allow you to use the features of social bookmarking to share information sources and discover those found by others, but has the added feature of allowing you to store a copy of the documents (it is available in a downloadable format, such as PDF).

- **Reference management** – these tools give you all the features of social bookmarking, but with the added functionality of formatting the resources details into a recognised referencing style, such as Harvard. Usually these references can then be downloaded and used a word-processing package. Examples include Zotero and Cite-U-Like. Mendeley also has this functionality.

Activity

Look at the list above.

- *Which sort of service meets your professional needs?*
- *Sign up for two of the services on their websites and experiment with using them.*
- *Think critically and creatively about how you could use this to support your professional development and enhance your skills.*

Summary

In this chapter you have learned:

- To consider your needs for digital information and media and start to think strategically.

- About definitions and frameworks of information literacy and how to apply them to your practice in the FE and Skills sector.

- About the different types of digital information and media available and the factors to consider when using them.

- To understand search processes and apply a suitable approach to your own practice.

- To appreciate the factors which affect our evaluation of resources in the digital age.

- How to organise your digital information and media resources and sources.

References and further reading

CILIP (2004) *Information Literacy – Definition.* Available at: http://www.cilip.org.uk/cilip/advocacy-campaigns-awards/advocacy-campaigns/information-literacy/information-literacy.

Education Scotland (2014) *Information and Critical Literacy.* Available at: http://www.educationscotland. gov.uk/informationliteracy/.

Hague, C and Payton, S (2010) *Digital Literacy Across the Curriculum: A FutureLab Handbook.* Available at: http://www.futurelab.org.uk/sites/default/files/Digital_Literacy_handbook_0.pdf.

Head, A J and Eisenberg, M B (2010) *Truth Be Told: How College Learners Evaluate and Use Information in the Digital Age.* Available at: http://projectinfolit.org/images/pdfs/pil_fall2010_ survey_fullreport1.pdf.

Hind, D and Moss, S (2011) *Employability Skills.* 2nd edn. Houghton le Spring: Business Education Publishers.

Irving, C and Crawford, J (2009) *National Information Literacy Framework for Scotland.* Available at: http://www.caledonianblogs.net/nilfs/.

Jisc (2005) *i-Skills.* Available at: http://www.jisc.ac.uk/publications/generalpublications/2005/pub_ sissdocs.

Jisc (2011) *Visitors and Residents: What Motivates Engagement with the Digital Information Environment?* Available at: http://www.jisc.ac.uk/whatwedo/projects/visitorsandresidents.aspx.

SCONUL (2011) *The SCONUL Seven Pillars of Information Literacy – Core Model.* Available at: http:// www.sconul.ac.uk/sites/default/files/documents/coremodel.pdf.

Secker, J and Coonan, E (2011) *A New Curriculum for Information Literacy: Curriculum and Supporting Documents.* Available at: http://newcurriculum.wordpress.com/project-reports-and-outputs/.

'Tony' (2009) 'BBC Watchdog: advice lines that exploit callers', *What Consumer Forum*, 12 May. Available at: http://whatconsumer.co.uk/forum/consumer-rights-television-programmes/5063-bbc-watchdog-advice-lines-exploit-callers.html.

UNESCO (2005) *The Alexandria Proclamation on Information Literacy*. Available at: http://www.
unesco.org/new/en/communication-and-information/access-to-knowledge/information-
literacy/.

White, D (2014) 'Visitors and residents: credibility'. Jisc Netskills YouTube video. Available at: http://
www.youtube.com/watch?v=kO569eknM6U&list=PLgO50IKGkqyaX21RaPiSpCKsf87O8S0Yv&feat
ure=share&index=2.

Wikipedia (2014) Available at: http://en.wikipedia.org/wiki/Wikipedia.

7 FORMING AND MANAGING A PROFESSIONAL DIGITAL IDENTITY

In this chapter you will learn:

- To consider what constitutes your digital identity.
- How to create and manage digital profiles.
- To consider the balance between personal and professional identities in the digital age.
- To choose appropriate digital services, tools and networks to showcase your skills, talents, knowledge and content.
- How to monitor your digital footprint and increase your digital capital.

Links to the Digitally Literate FE and Skills Teacher Framework

5.   *Forms and manages a professional digital identity and uses it to engage professionally.*

5.1   *Forms and manages a professional digital identity.*

5.2   *Contributes to, and engages in, digital communities in order to establish and maintain a digital identity.*

Your digital identity

The digital identity we each have is made up of all the profiles, interactions, communications and digital content we have online. This enormous amount of data amasses over time as we use the Web and is stored by all the different services we use, the non-secured and unhidden parts becoming findable and reusable by anyone. As professional teachers in the FE and Skills sector, our presence on the Web is becoming more and more important, especially in times of rapid change and uncertainty. Therefore we need to make sure that our digital identities enable us to do the following:

- Demonstrate our professional and personal interests.

- Grow our network of contacts.

- Establish and maintain a voice in the conversations which shape our sector and its work.

- Discover new knowledge and content and interact with it.

- Showcase our own talents, achievements, skills, creativity and critical thinking.

- Curate, manage and disseminate digital content.

You may be doing some, none or all of these things, and some of them may not mean that much at this stage. Through this chapter each shall be explored with opportunities for you to consider the best way to take control of your digital identity and use it to your advantage.

What constitutes a digital identity?

The digital identity we each have is broadly made up of profiles and content. Profiles can be thought of as the accounts we have on networks, services and tools and content is what we produce using the profile.

Profiles

Not all profiles are created equal. Sometimes we put more effort into one profile than others depending upon our level of engagement with that network, service or tool (see also Chapter 3). The amount of information we are able to put on to the profile can also differ between technologies, with some allowing much more than others. Depending upon the technology you may share any of the following pieces of information through your profiles:

- **Personal details** – such as name, contact details (personal or work), employment history, skills, qualifications, photograph, location.

- **Our connections** – depending upon the technology this can be followers of us, those we follow, friends, family and colleagues.

- **Group memberships** – this can be groups we have joined (whether membership and professional based or just a group of likeminded individuals).

Content

The content element of our digital identity is formed by the following interactions:

- **Likes** – a wide variety of media, pages, and other content we have stipulated an interest in/approval of through 'Likes'.

- **Posts and comments** – through the language we use when posting and the comments we make on others' posts, we express our thoughts, ideas, beliefs, opinions.

- **Shared content** – this is content you discover online and share to your connections. Sharing implies that you have consumed the content. Usually comments are provided alongside the share to indicate the purpose for sharing it. The purpose is usually to agree with it, disagree with it, critique it or to stimulate debate.

- **Produced, uploaded and published content, and contributions** – this can be a wide variety of resources you create, including lesson activities, learning resources, reports, articles, videos and audio clips. It can also be edits you make and contributions you provide to information and debates on networks, forums, blogs and wikis.

The list of interactions above has been ordered to reflect activities which demonstrate 'low engagement' through 'Likes', through to 'high engagement' through 'Produced, uploaded and published content, and contributions'. When people find our content they may judge our commitment and engagement with the subject matter and/or our knowledge, skills and expertise through how much of each interaction type we do and the way in which we do it. (See Chapter 3 for more on the development of your levels of engagement around your digital interactions.)

Both our profiles and the content we put online say a lot about who we are, what we are interested in, our beliefs, our professional interests, and our knowledge, skills and experience. Very often people say that what they put online is only a small part of 'who they are', or that they 'are a different person online', therefore making the distinction between their digital identity and their 'real world' identity. However, there is an increasingly blurred line between the two, with professional networking, opinion forming and connection making happening as much in digital environments as it does in 'real world' environments. This means that those we wish to influence and network with could start to form a picture about our personality, our professional status and ranking, and our knowledge, skills and expertise, all before ever meeting us in the 'real world'. In some cases, this could affect job opportunities and career prospects.

It is therefore wise to take control and ownership of your digital identity and make sure that you present yourself as you would want to be interpreted.

Personal and private digital identities

Taking control and ownership of your digital identity in order to increase your professional presence is possible with planning and effort. In relation to this, we look at how you can engage in professional digital communities, and start to showcase your knowledge, skills and talents later in this chapter. First, though, we need to consider if there is a difference between a professional and personal digital identity.

As a part of creating and managing their digital identity, some people decide to separate their professional and private lives by having multiple social network accounts, securing some social network accounts so that they cannot be seen by anyone other than their connections, using pseudonyms, or by embedding the statement 'All views are my own and do not represent those of my employer'. There may be good reasons for taking one or more of these approaches, and sometimes this is based on employer policy, worries about personal details being seen by learners, and by the need for a private digital space where friends and family are the only connections.

An alternative view is that your personality and interests are just as much a part of your professional identity as your 'work' persona is. Everyone is, after all, a complex individual with many different parts to their character. These personality traits can be seen when we interact face to face in 'real life', and our personality undoubtedly allows us to form connection with people we meet in a professional context. Therefore, it is important that we demonstrate some of our personalities when we interact professionally online. After all, we do not have just one formal communication style in real life, so why should we feel the need to adopt just one for many and diverse digital interactions? As Dr Claire Warwick from University College London (2011) stated in a recent lecture on the use of Twitter and digital identities, 'we all have different registers and use them online, and [we] make no apologies for that!'

Whether you decide to separate your personal and professional digital identities, or fuse them, is a decision for the individual based upon their professional judgement and needs. However, it is important to remember that demonstrating some of your personal interests and parts of your personality in a professional content may actually help you to engage with connections and will increase people's interest in what you have to say. Give other users a reason to follow you and engage with your content!

Monitoring your digital footprints

The term 'digital footprint' is sometimes used synonymously with the term digital identity, but there is a subtle difference between the two. The 'trail' of data we generate when using our profiles and interacting with digital content forms our digital footprint, so while we consciously form a digital identity through our creation of profiles and interactions with digital content, we unconsciously generate a digital footprint in the process. Our digital footprint contains a wealth of data, including details about our location, the devices/browsers/apps we use, the dates and times of our interactions, the duration of an interaction, the frequency of visits we make to an app, service, website, keywords and tags, and much more depending on the technology and how we used it.

This data is frequently stored, exchanged and used by and between digital technologies for the purpose of creating a more personalised experience for us on the Web, and for delivering more relevant results and content to us in search engines, advertisements and suggestions of other useful content. This could have both advantages and disadvantages depending upon whether the data generated is for a perceived positive or negative use.

You can often find ways to turn off the collection of certain data in the settings of the digital technology and sometimes you are given the choice as to whether you want certain data to be shared and stored, and for what purposes it can be used. However, it is quite difficult to make all of the security settings 'airtight', across all of your different networks, tools, services, apps and devices.

Example

Jim keeps his use of social media split between personal and professional uses – with his Facebook account for 'personal use' – interacting with close friends and family, sharing entertainment content and photographs taken in his leisure time – and his Twitter account for 'professional use' – interacting with work colleagues and other education professionals, sharing articles, media and links to resources relevant to teaching his subject area, business. Recently, Jim was photographed on a night out drinking a pint of beer by a friend-of-a-friend, which was subsequently uploaded to Facebook, labelled 'what a business teacher does best' and Jim was tagged within it. Jim was not concerned by this, as his Facebook security settings mean that none of his Facebook content can be seen by anyone other than his friends. However, a few months later Jim searched for his name plus 'business teacher' within a search engine to find that this photo came up on the first page of an image search. Upon investigation of his privacy settings, he realised that his settings do not protect him against the settings of others, and that it was a friend who uploaded the picture and tagged him within it. The tag of his profile, plus the use of the term 'business teacher', has generated data which can be used by search engines to index the content. Jim is now concerned that this picture, although not offensive, does not portray him in an unprofessional manner and is not detrimental to the digital identity he wishes to have.

Due to the difficulty in being able to completely manage what appears on the Web about you, it is important to put concerns over security, reputation and professionalism into perspective and learn to use data to your advantage, rather than spending too much time 'policing' content. In the example of Jim, the photo is not detrimental to his character, identity or professional standing, as it shows that he is sociable, has a life outside work and projects a personality. It helps that this is not the only content about him online, as most of the other content on him in the public domain is about his professional life. In the next section of this chapter we look at how and where you can showcase your knowledge, skills and abilities in order to boost your digital identity and consider how you can optimise the data you generate in order to optimise your discoverability.

Activity

Find the terms and conditions of usage for a digital technology you use regularly (e.g. a social network/media service, search engine, app, Website or mobile device) and look for references to 'your information', 'personal details' and 'usage data' and for how it is collected, shared and used.

- For what purposes could this data be used?

- Does it explain how you can alter your privacy settings?

- If there are some data settings you cannot alter, but you do not want to stop using the digital technology, what steps could you take to ensure the data generated is used positively and to your advantage?

Showcasing through a portfolio approach

If utilised and managed effectively, the sum of your digital identity can become a digital portfolio stretching across the Web, showcasing your professional knowledge, skills, experience and achievements, as well as your commitment to continuous professional development (CPD), creative abilities, and critical thinking and judgement. Tristram Hooley (2012) outlines a list of seven Cs we must all understand and do with digital technologies in order to manage our careers more effectively. The seven Cs are: changing, collecting, critiquing, connecting, communicating, creating and curating.

Being proficient in these Cs is key to being a digitally literate professional and they are covered throughout this book, but in particular we are focusing on connecting, communicating, creating and curating in this chapter. By participating in the interactions detailed below you will gain a better understanding of using these networks, tools and services, and will begin to establish your position as a digital professional.

1. Participate in networks

First, you need to make sure that you are participating in the networks and other platforms most widely used by teachers and other education professionals. These can be general or subject specific. Twitter and LinkedIn are two accessible social networks used by many education professionals. The conversational structure of Twitter means that you can easily find conversations on specific topics, read through them and participate when you are ready and have knowledge, resources and experiences to share on them. Try searching for #UKFEchat to read through the discussion ongoing about the FE topic of the week. New topics start on Thursday evenings, when the main conversation takes place. The *TES* has published a guide to #UKFEchat which can be downloaded from their website (*TES*, 2014). LinkedIn is more like Facebook in structure, where users post a status or share content either with their connections or into groups they are part of. The difference is that you can only connect with people you have things in common with, such as employer, qualifications or membership of a group. With both Twitter and Facebook, you will find that the more you participate, the more connections you will make. Some of those connections can become very useful contacts.

Forums can also be used as a way to engage in professional debate, discover resources and gain new knowledge and perspectives. Forums contain 'threads' on different topics, some of which may have been started by the owners of the forum, while others will have been started by users. They can be based around a debate on or discussion of a particular issue, or may start with a question being posed. *TES* forums is one of the biggest forums for education professionals, but many others exist across a range of subject specialist areas. Type 'further education forum' or your subject specialism and the word 'forum' into a search engine to identify relevant forums. If you are unable to find any relevant forums, or find that content on them is out of date, try looking at Twitter and LinkedIn groups, as many forum-style discussions on professional topics have moved to those platforms in recent years.

Tips for contributing:

- **Find your voice** – what are your professional interests? Find a balance between your formal and informal writing styles – this is a conversation, but a professional conversation.

- **State your intentions** – make it clear whether you are speaking from opinion, experience or evidence.

- **Give credit** – where relevant, mention other users by tagging them in to your posts and share or quote their content.

- **Tag everything** – use keywords. Hash-tagged keywords are best known for being a feature of Twitter, but actually work across a wide range of social networks. Using keywords can make it easier for your content to be discovered by humans, but also to be automatically indexed by bots for search engines and by curation and storytelling services. Do not over use hash tagging though, only use where there are genuinely useful keywords relevant to your content.

Activity

Observe professional conversations taking place on social networks, in groups and forums.

- *What are the main topics being discussed?*

- *What sort of information and resources are being shared (e.g. articles, videos, documents, learning resources)?*

- *Record what you have learned. What digital tools could you use to gather and store this information?*

- *How can you participate? Do you have anything you can input into the discussion?*

2. Disseminate your content and knowledge

In Chapter 5 we looked at getting creative with digital technologies and using digital tools to create your own resources and content. Here we discuss the outlets in which you can share your creativity and thereby boost your digital identity.

Many different types of services exist, into which you contribute your content. The following services and tools could be considered depending upon the nature of your content:

- **Open educational resources** (OERs) – these services allow teachers to upload and share resources they have created, which can then be accessed, downloaded and reused by other teachers. The resources available through OERs can be in the form of documents, audio and video resources, or learning objects. Jorum is the most well known and useful OER platform for the FE and Skills sector, while OER Commons has a more international focus.

- **Presentation networks** – these services and tools allow you to upload and/or create presentations for others to find, watch and reuse. As well as hosting and creation functionality, they also tend to have many social media features, such as the ability to share and discover content, like and comment on presentations and the ability to collaborate on presentation projects. Two of the most popular examples are Prezi and SlideShare.

- **Blogs and podcasts** – blogs are websites that contain regularly posted and updated content on anything the blog owner wants/needs to disseminate. Individual blog posts can be anything, from short pieces of information through to full length articles. All articles are given a date and time stamp as they are published and the most recent appears first. We look at some examples below in 'creating a hub'. Podcasts are similar to blogs, in that they are regularly published with a date and time stamp, but these are mainly designed to hold audio and video content. This can be set to download regularly and then be uploaded to a digital media player, MP3 player or mobile device. The word *podcast* comes from 'ipod' and 'broadcast'. iTunes is a very popular service for finding and downloading podcasts, with podcast creators able to use iTunes to host or just aggregate their podcasts. Search for 'education' to find examples of the types of podcast available. Both can be useful if you want to release information on a subject/topic over time, and can be a good way of recording and disseminating knowledge and skills as you gain and develop them.

- **Video and photo services** – if you have created image-based content such as photographs, pictures and videos, then there are many services you can use to host and disseminate this content. While anyone can post this content to social media sites, you often lose rights and control over your content when you do. That's why many dedicated services exist for video and photo sharing, which are used by professionals. Flickr and Photobucket are very popular for image and photo sharing, as they contain a range of professional tools and allow for licences to be applied to content (see Chapter 9 for more information on licensing). YouTube is the most popular tool for video sharing and has much of the same functionality as Flickr and Photobucket. Wikimedia Commons allows for the upload, licensing and dissemination of both audio and visual content.

- **Wikis** – wikis are digital encyclopaedias to which anyone, or members and users of a community, can contribute. Wikipedia is the most popular example of a mass, multidisciplinary wiki, but many also exist that are more niche. Wikispaces and PBWorks are examples of popular wiki-hosting services. If you want to share and contribute your knowledge on a subject, then adding to wikis might be a good way forward.

- **Academic, professional and trade journals** – journals did start life as a digital medium, in fact some have been published in various forms for more than a century. Journals continue, though, to be the most prestigious, rigorous and respected form of publishing on a subject, and they have successfully transitioned to being a primarily digital medium. The following distinctions can be made, depending upon the type of content to be published:

  o For any content based upon research, and/or that adheres to strict principles of scholarship, academic journals could be the best place to publish. This could include articles on research findings, reviews of research on a particular subject and book reviews. Open access journals are freely published online, so can provide maximum exposure and availability for your content. They still follow the principles of academic rigour though, and most are peer reviewed. The *Directory of Open Access Journals* (DOAJ) lists the majority of open access journals worldwide.

  o Professional and trade journals are used by those within an industry or discipline to keep up to date with new developments and news within that industry. If you have practical knowledge and information to share, then these may be the best place to publish it. Search on your subject specialism to identify professional and trade journals, or ask your library/learning resources centres.

Wherever you decide to publish your content, make sure that you consider the disadvantages of a variety of platforms and publications before doing so. Also consider the policy of your institution on doing so and read about licensing and copyright in Chapter 9 before going ahead.

3. Create a 'hub'

One way to increase the presence of your profiles and content is to create a 'hub' in which you can bring everything together. This can then be used as a 'landing page' where other Web users can discover more about you and connect with you and your content on multiple platforms. As everything is linked, it will become more discoverable to users and enable search engines to better prioritise and index your content. Over time, this should have a positive effect on your digital identity, with professional content rising higher in search results.

A good way to think of your hub is as a professional space which you control, and also as a digital CV and portfolio. Therefore you need to decide whether creating and managing a hub is right for you and how you would approach it. Consider the following:

- **How many professional profiles do you have on social media?** If you are active on multiple networks or want to increase the prominence of your social media profiles then a hub is right for you.

- **Have you contributed content to the Web or are your achievements recorded/acknowledged somewhere on the Web?** A hub will allow you to link to this content and promote it widely.

- **Do you need to learn any further digital skills before creating a hub?** This may be a good time to take stock of what you have learnt about using digital technologies so far and consider what you still need to learn/improve on and how you will do this.

If you decide to create a hub for your profiles, content and achievements, you need to consider which software would best suit your needs. Basically, we are talking about creating a website. The easiest way to do this is to use one of the many services and tools that allow you to create a basic website and name it with a URL which allows you some flexibility in name. These tools and services are called content management systems (CMS) and there are a lot in existence. Some of the more popular examples are WIX, Moonfruit and Weebly. These services do not require you to have any coding skills or knowledge of Hypertext Mark-up Language (HTML) and instead allow you to add text, images, videos and other content to a choice of templates. However, these are mainly used for commercial purposes, such as setting up Web shops, or promoting businesses and services.

Many professionals instead use a blogging platform as a CMS, and many of the more popular blogging platforms provide all the capability and tools you need to host a functioning website. Wordpress, Edublogs and Blogger are three of the most popular platforms used by education professionals. The main advantage of using a blogging platform is that you can have full website capability and a blog built into your hub from the beginning, as integrating a blog into an existing website at a later stage can be quite complicated and is not always available for free on some platforms. Before making the decision you need to decide if a blog is required and if blogging is for you.

Blogging is useful if you have longer messages, information and content to be shared than is appropriate and possible on social networks, where length is very often restricted. Blog posts are time and date stamped when you post them, are not restricted by length, and are not limited to the amount of media you can embed into them. Through blogging you can share reports on events and conferences, reviews of educational resources, articles about research you have carried out, a teaching method you have tried or your considered thoughts on a professional issue. Readers can then like, reply to, link to, or share your blog posts and can follow your blog to receive notification when you post. This is usually by email or really simple syndication (RSS).

Whichever CMS platform you decide to use to build your hub, consider putting the following on to your hub in order to get started:

- **About page.** This gives basic details about you and what the website is for. You shouldn't lay this out as a CV, but you should put your name, what you do and what your professional interests are as a minimum. It is advisable never to put personal contact details on there, such as home and mobile phone numbers and your home address. You should also consider if it is appropriate to mention which institution you work for. If in doubt, check if your institution has a social media policy (this would cover personal blogs and websites).

- **Social feeds/buttons.** If you have a profile, page or group on any of the popular social networks you should be able to obtain a short piece of code which allows you to embed a stream, or feed, of posts from that account. You can also obtain code to embed 'like', 'join' or 'connect' buttons on your website. To find the required code and instructions for using it look in the 'settings' area, the 'help' area or frequently asked questions (FAQs) section. Search for 'social buttons' or 'embed code'. Then look for the same sections on the CMS you are using to find out how and where to paste the content into your website.

- **Links to/embedded content.** If you have content on social media platforms, such as photo collections on Flickr or videos on YouTube, you can obtain a short piece of code to embed the media directly into your Web pages or into blog posts. Use the same method, as described above for social feeds and buttons to do this.

- **Blog.** Adding a blog to your website and posting regularly can really increase the number of visitors to it and search engine to bots to discover and index it. This is sometimes described as Web traffic. Blogging can also increase your digital skills, confidence in your subject knowledge and abilities, and allow you to make new connections. See above for how to create a blog.

Optimising your digital identity

If we are to start taking more control over our digital identity and footprints, we must consider how they are going to be discovered by potential viewers/users. Most users will search in either a search engine or within a social network to either find content on a particular subject, using subject keywords, or to find the profiles and content of a particular person, using either just their name or a combination of name and subject keywords. Therefore, if you have content that you want to be discovered on a particular subject, or if you want to increase your reputation and standing in a particular area it is beneficial to optimise where you and your content appear in search engine results, i.e. to get higher within search results. This is referred to as search engine optimisation (SEO) and a large industry exists around it, providing businesses with the means to make their content more discoverable, with organisations spending large marketing budgets on doing this. For individual professionals though, optimisation of the discoverability of your digital identity does not need to cost anything, although it will require time, effort and thought. The benefits could be great though, as you become part of the professional discourse, grow your network and see you content being reused and receiving recognition.

The easiest way to do this is by tagging all your posts and content with keywords. Depending on the platform, this may either be in the form of tags (most common in blogs, forums and content networks) or hash tags (most common on social network and media sites). Combined with the linking and re-linking of your content between your profiles and on your hub, this will all make your content more discoverable to search engine bots and increase its ranking within search engine results.

The importance of the three main search engines in the formation of our digital identities should not be underestimated, as Google, Bing and Yahoo! consistently host the majority of the UK's search traffic. As a result, it could be argued that only the profiles and content which appear in the first two pages of search engine results really matter, as few people look beyond the first two pages. This means that your 'worth' as a professional could be decided by these results, and could potentially affect your career prospects and professional status. This new 'currency' can be thought of as your 'digital capital', or you worth in terms of your digital identity. More on the idea of digital capital can be found in White (2014), where using the term with students is explored as they begin to formulate their digital identity and plan for their careers.

The power and dominance of search engines in shaping our digital identities have been recognised by the European Union, who's Court of Justice accepted the pivotal role search engines play in making information about us discoverable and ruled that we each have a 'right to be forgotten' by search engines (European Commission, 2014). This entitles those who feel that information about them that is prominent and ranks highly in search engine results can request for search engines to remove links and indexing of this content by filling in a form provided by search engines, and they should comply where the information is 'inaccurate, inadequate, irrelevant or excessive'.

Search for yourself and analyse the results. Would you rate your digital capital as high or low?

Activity

Forming a digital impression:

- *Work with a colleague and search for each other's profiles using a search engine.*
  - *Are they easy to find/findable at all?*
  - *What keywords do you need to use to find them?*

(Continued)

(Continued)

- *If you find nothing try searching for them on Facebook, Twitter, LinkedIn and other social networks/media they use.*

- *Judging them only by the profiles and content you find, how would you describe that person on both a personal and professional level?*

- *Share your results with each other.*

- *Reflect on the feedback:*

  o *What stands out as being something you think is extremely representative of your identity and/or highlights you as a good professional teacher? How can you increase content of this nature?*

  o *What stands out as being something that you think is extremely unrepresentative of your identity, or could give others a false impression of you, and does not highlight your professionalism? How can you decrease content of this nature?*

What to do next?

To progress your skills you could consider doing any of the following:

- Purchase a domain and hosting.

- Learn HTML – the language of the Web – in order to further develop and customise your personal website. You could also use a more sophisticated CMS, such as JOOMLA. This will give you more freedom on the design of your website, but the tools you use require an advanced level of understanding and knowledge, and understanding of HTML and CSS would also be required.

Summary

In this chapter you have learned:

- To consider what constitutes your digital identity.

- How to create and manage digital profiles.

- To consider the balance between personal and professional identities in the digital age.

- To choose appropriate digital services, tools and networks to showcase your skills, talents, knowledge and content.

- How to monitor your digital footprint and increase your digital capital.

References and further reading

Cambridge, D (2010) *E-portfolios for Lifelong Learning and Assessment*. San Francisco: Jossey-Bass.

European Commission (2014) *Factsheet on the 'Right to be Forgotten' Ruling* (C-131/12). Available at: http://ec.europa.eu/justice/data-protection/files/factsheets/factsheet_data_protection_en.pdf/.

Hooley, T (2012) 'How the Internet changed career: framing the relationship between career development and online technologies', *Journal of the National Institute for Career Education and Counselling*, 29 October: 3–12.

Poore, M (2013) *Using Social Media in the Classroom: A Best Practice Guide*. London: Sage.

TES (2014) *The UKFEchat Guide*. Available at: http://digital.tes.co.uk/FECHAT/html5/index.html?page=1.

Warwick, C (2011) 'Great 2 meet u IRL :-) Twitter and digital identity (17 March 2011)', in UCL Lunch Hour Lectures (YouTube video). Available at: http://youtu.be/tJ59Md8KSDE.

White, J P (2014) 'What is your digital capital?', Teach Digital Literacy blog, 24 November. Available at: http://teachdigitalliteracy.com/2014/11/24/what-is-your-digital-capital/.

Search #UKFEchat on Twitter to read the discussions that go on here. If you feel comfortable with the platform and have a comment or point to make on the discussion, use the hash tag and join in.

8 DIGITAL SAFETY, SECURITY AND CITIZENSHIP

In this chapter you will learn:

- About the concept of digital citizenship and the rights and responsibilities we have in digital environments.
- What your legal, ethical and professional duties are in relation to digital safety and digital security
- About cyberbullying, grooming and pressurisation online, and how to recognise and respond to them.
- How to manage your communications with learners in digital environments and professional conduct.
- About digital data, and how to keep it safe and secure.

Links to the Digitally Literate FE and Skills Teacher Framework

6. *Understands and leads on digital safety, security, ethical and legal responsibilities, and citizenship.*

6.1 *Understands digital safety and security concerns, and is aware of safeguarding responsibilities and procedures.*

6.3 *Understands the definition of digital citizenship and recognises the rights and responsibilities we each have in digital environments.*

In this chapter and the next, we will consider issues with a legal, ethical and moral dimension. The information on specific legal duties was accurate at the time of writing, but you should check to see if anything has changed or been amended. The other advice given is, like the rest of this book, designed to enable your critical thinking on the topics covered, while relating the issues of the use of digital technologies to the FE and Skills sector. These chapters are not intended to be comprehensive legal and professional advice. If in any doubt you should consult in-house experts, such as your human resources department and safeguarding officer, or seek guidance and advice from the sector professional body or your trade union. Sources of further information, advice and guidance are referenced throughout.

Safety and security in the FE and Skills sector

As professionals in education, our ethical and legal responsibilities are far reaching, with the following areas being at the forefront of every teacher's mind and every institution's priorities:

- The safeguarding of all students and staff from bullying, abuse, discrimination and unsafe situations. For learners under the age of 18 and in vulnerable groups, specific legal duties exist for FE institutions to safeguard and protect them from such behaviour and situations.

- The need to promote and ensure equality and to understand and respect diversity, across the institution and beyond. Specific legal duties exist which ensure educational institutions and other public services take an active role in making sure their practices and the way in which they teach are inclusive of all learners and respect diversity.

- The need to ensure quality and compliance with legislation and regulation (such as complying with safeguarding legislation, copyright law and regulations from government bodies, such as Ofsted) and the needs of other interested bodies (such as guidelines set out by professional bodies, charities and other organisations).

- To provide a subject specialist-based curriculum, but also to provide learning around, and give guidance on, wider social and pastoral issues and teach learners to understand situations and take responsibility for their conduct within them.

These responsibilities existed before digital technologies were such an integral part of our everyday lives and of education. As the uptake and usage of digital technologies have increased exponentially over the past decade though, so have concerns about digital safety and security, and some of the issues above, which were previously only experienced and dealt with in the physical world, have become very big issues in the digital world.

To respond to and plan for these issues, we need to understand our rights and responsibilities, both as teachers in the FE and Skills sector and as citizens using digital technologies. In doing so, we will have the knowledge and understanding to perform our duties correctly, to educate learners to be safe and responsible and to identify and deal with problematic situations as they arise.

Being a digital citizen

The way in which digital safety, security, ethics and legality are governed, administered and taught in your institution will depend upon the type of learners it primarily serves and the programmes it delivers. In most FE and Skills institutions there will be policies to cover IT equipment and network usage, and there may also be policies and guidance on professional conduct online, social networking, dealing with cyberbullying and harassment, and use of digital content for learning and teaching. Some institutions and programmes, especially those tailored for learners under the age of 19, will have set pastoral teaching and personal tutoring time, in which digital safety and security may be covered along with other topics such as personal safety, respect for the self and others, financial stability, healthy lifestyles, democracy and accessing public services. Very often this is collectively known as citizenship education.

The term 'digital citizen' has arisen to describe the people we are when in digital environments and when using digital technologies, and how as members of a 'society' when online, we understand our rights, responsibilities and duties, and act in an manner appropriate to them. A traditional understanding of citizenship encompasses understanding and living within a set of particular values, while at the same time understanding the legal responsibilities and ethical duties you have as a citizen, as well as the rights you have. Depending upon the society, its political system, cultures, customs, heritage and belief system(s), a 'citizen' and how they behave may be different across borders. The digital world has few, if any, of these borders, and so a digital citizen is not naturally bound by such restrictions, and therefore may not observe the same rules as they would in the physical world. The individual's perceptions of the digital world as a 'place' (or not) may also inform how they behave and conduct their activities online. Therefore, there may not be shared values between uses of digital technologies, such as those set out in Chapter 3.

Example

White and LeCornu's (2011) visitors and residents distinction can be used to help us consider to what extent someone may view themselves as a digital citizen (see definition above) in different scenarios (see Chapter 3 for a discussion of this concept). With this in mind, consider the two examples below:

Sam recently attended a friend's wedding and has been sent a link to the official photographer's collection of photos on a website. Sam follows the link and quickly skims through the images. He finds two he really likes, saves them to his PC using the print screen button and exits the website. One he prints off and the other he uploads to his Facebook profile. He notices that there is a small watermark in one corner, but decides that this is unimportant, as it is hardly noticeable.

Meanwhile, Chloe also attended the wedding and also follows the link to the website. The website is one that Chloe has used before, and being into photography herself, knows that this is a site in which photographers display their work with watermarks, from which high-quality prints can be ordered for personal use. She quickly notices that there is a copyright statement present which states that the images on the website are the copyright of the photographer and should not be distributed or copied without the express consent of the photographer. It also states that they are displayed on the website in low resolution and with watermark for the purpose of selling high-quality prints of the images only. Chloe respects this, and proceeds to choose three images to have produced as high-quality prints. She logs into the website and pays for the prints. Later that day, Chloe logs into Facebook to see that Sam has uploaded one of the images to his profile. It is of very low quality and features the watermark. She notices that the bride has commented that she is upset that Sam has done this, as they have a good relationship with the photographer and he is likely to be at the least offended by Sam's actions, and may pursue the matter further. Chloe knows that Sam is unlikely to see this message, as he rarely uses Facebook, so it may be at least a few days before he notices the message. She also knows that he is not likely to realise the implications of what he has done. She decides to phone him and explain the situation.

Activity

Think about how Sam and Chloe have each acted:

- *Which person has a better of understanding of their own digital citizenship and why?*

- *Chloe is more of a resident on the image-sharing website and Facebook than Sam, who appears to be more of a visitor. Does this have a bearing on their engagement with the websites and their possible understanding of them?*

Activity

Make a list of what you believe your digital rights and responsibilities are. Think about the different ways in which you use digital technologies and the different activities you engage with in digital environments (consumption, comment, communication and/or production) – some of your rights and responsibilities may differ depending upon the activity. As you read through the rest of this chapter and the next, edit and update the list as you learn more about specific rights and responsibilities. You may want to use this list as the basis of an activity with your students in which they work together to produce a set of guidelines for interacting online.

Legal and professional responsibilities of the teacher and FE institution

In the UK, any person working with children who are defined as being anyone under the age of 18, and/or with vulnerable adults, which includes those with learning difficulties and recognised disabilities, has a legal duty of care towards learners within these groups. This includes safeguarding and protecting these learners from harm and reporting areas for concern to the appropriate persons. The wider organisation is legally required to have appropriate safeguarding policies and procedures. This usually includes nominating or appointing a Safeguarding Officer who has responsibilities for investigating all concerns raised by staff and students and in liaising with external bodies to take further action if required, such as police and social services departments. Set out in the Children Act 1989, this legal duty applies to everyone working in education who has contact with children and vulnerable adults (the Children Act, 1989). This could potentially include all staff working within the organisation, including teachers, lecturers, assessors, invigilators, managers and support staff. Additionally, your own institution may extend the duties of staff to ensure safeguarding of all learners and staff through institutional policy. You should seek guidance from within your institution to find out what specific duties you have to all learners.

In the digital age, the responsibilities for the safety and security of learners extend beyond the physical walls of an institution, as many learners are interacting and communicating through digital technologies before, during and after classes. While the Children Act 1989 is the most often-cited piece of legislation with regards to safety issues in education, the potential for, and nature of, incidents and issues around safety and security is increased in digital environments. Teachers therefore need to be aware of an increasingly growing number of issues and possible responses, as well as the legal duties they have and the legal status of some issues learners and teachers may become involved in. As issues are explored below, relevant legislation is cited and discussed.

FE and Skills institutions with learners under the age of 18 have the explicit duty of planning, at the Governor level, for the institution's operations to be 'exercised with a view to safeguarding and promoting the welfare of children receiving education or training at the institution' (Education Act 2002, s. 175, in Department for Schools, Children and Families and Department for Innovation, Universities and Skills, 2009: 9).

Cyberbullying

Cyberbullying as a term has grown in usage over the past decade to describe bullying that takes place in digital environments. Hoechsmann and Poyntz (2012: 145) define cyberbullying as 'the use of new media to circulate hurtful or abusive texts about or images of others, and covers both the act of bullying and the circumstance of victimhood'. This is a good definition, but 'new media' is a term sometimes associated directly with social media, whereas cyberbullying can take place across a wide variety of media, networks, websites, platforms, apps and devices, in fact using just about any digital technology. Poore's (2013: 189) definition is therefore much more succinct, while addressing all scenarios: '[cyberbullying is] any hostile act directed towards another person that occurs using digital technology.'

The problem of cyberbullying is increasing with a number of reports highlight how much bullying learners, and young people in particular, face in digital environments. In 2013, the helpline ChildLine reported an increase of 87 per cent in the number of calls they receive about cyberbullying in just one year (ChildLine, 2013) and the anti-bullying charity Ditch the Label recently published research reporting that 62 per cent of the 13–25-year-olds they asked had received 'nasty' messages via smartphone apps, 47 per cent had received 'nasty' comments on their profiles and 42 per cent had received comments which were hate-based, such as being homophobic or racist (Ditch the Label, 2015).

Learners are not the only group to be targets for cyberbullying though. In 2015 NASUWT – the teachers' union – reported that 60 per cent of respondents to their annual survey said they had been victims of cyberbullying by pupils and parents (NASUWT, 2015). Similarly, the Department for Education (2014a) reported that 21 per cent of all teachers have reported 'having derogatory comments posted about them on social media sites from both parents and children'. The issue is therefore a widespread problem affecting all educational sectors and institutions.

Cyberbullying, like traditional bullying, could take many forms, but it is likely to fit into one of these categories or a mixture of them:

- **Insults, offensive use of language, abusive language and hate-based comments aimed at individual or groups** – about anything to which a person takes offence, but remember some characteristics, such as race, sex, sexual orientation and religion, are protected characteristics as defined by the Equality Act 2010. Abuse of this nature could lead to criminal prosecution.

- **Threats and blackmail** – this can include threats of physical violence, but could also include threats to share secrets, personal details or images and videos if the victim does not do something for the bully. This can quickly become blackmail. In some circumstances this could lead to criminal prosecution if the threats were found to have been made with serious intent, or if the recipient felt at risk.

- **Sharing of photographs, images and videos of a person without their consent/ without their knowledge** – this could be bullying if this is a photo taken and/or shared without or against the person's consent, or if it is used as a means to attack or belittle a person based upon their characteristics. Criminal prosecution could occur if inappropriate images of children are shared.

- **'Naming and shaming' and airing personal grievances** – this involves a person posting comments about a person where they have a personal grudge against or issue with that person.

- **Targeting and 'trolling'** – this involves 'sitting' on social networks/media, forums, blogs etc. to prey on a specific person or group for the purpose of relentless bullying, to attack them or to encourage them to partake in self-abusing behaviour. This is usually done using a pseudonym or anonymously.

- **Accusations and rumours** – this involves posting or sharing posts about individuals which may or may not be true. The comments could be libellous and open to legal challenge if they cannot be backed up.

As cyberbullying can take many forms, it is sometimes missed or some incidents are not taken as seriously as others. Cyberbullying in all its forms can have a devastating effect on its victims and it is hard to predict and estimate how much certain types of bullying will affect an individual. Remember, no two people are alike, and will react differently from others.

Activity

Search online for stories in the media about incidents of cyberbullying in order to get an overview of the nature of incidents which occur, and to keep up to date with new digital technologies being used as mediums for cyberbullying. Most search engines have a 'news' search function which will find freely available news articles, or your institution's library may subscribe to a news database giving access to a wide range of articles from newspapers and news services. There are many high-profile examples of cyberbullying taking place which have become news stories you may wish to search for and read about.

Visit my blog to read a post about two examples which received a lot of media attention in 2013: http://teachdigitalliteracy.com/2013/08/11/in-the-news-1/ (White, 2013). The case of the cyberbullying of historian Mary Beard highlights that consequences for cyberbullies can include criminal prosecution, but the cases of vulnerable teenagers bullied and abused to the point of suicide show the devastating effect cyberbullying can have on victims and their families.

Bullying through digital technologies can occur solely online in digital environments or may take place in both the physical and digital world. The availability of recording equipment through mobile devices, such as still and video cameras and audio recording, means that the opportunities to capture embarrassing moments and potentially use them for bullying in digital environments are greater than ever before. As the Department for Schools, Children and Families and Department for Innovation, Universities and Skills (2009) pointed out, this may lead to 'Situations [being] deliberately engineered in order to photograph someone in a humiliating way'. Incidents may also occur which begin in digital environments, but move into the physical world and turn into incidents in classrooms or elsewhere in the institution. It is therefore important to be vigilante for possible signs of problems and to realise that some incidents which occur may have deeper causes and long-standing issues which stretch beyond what has happened in college.

How to tackle cyberbullying

The first step is to ensure that a culture exists which takes cyberbullying seriously and encourages the reporting of it. Most colleges will have policy and guidance on how to deal with incidents of cyberbullying, and it may be appropriate to discuss the issue with your learners and let them know that incidents of cyberbullying, as with all bullying and abusive behaviour, are taken seriously by the institution and can be reported to you and colleagues. Sometimes posters and information on the institution's website or VLE will be displayed for learners to read.

The Department for Children, Schools and Families and Department for Innovation, Universities and Skills' (2009) advice for dealing with bullying, including cyberbullying, lists the following steps to be worked through:

- Make the victim safe.

- Stop the bullying and change the bully's behaviour.

- Make clear to every learner that bullying is unacceptable.

- Learn lessons from the experience that can be applied in the future.

Teaching learners to understand what constitutes cyberbullying and to think critically before engaging in any activities which could be cyberbullying is extremely important and you do not need to wait until a situation occurs before teaching these concepts. The most important skill to develop is how to identify and support victims of cyberbullying and find solutions to their issues. The most obvious signs that a learner is having problems are:

- Changes in mood, behaviour, health, appearance and attitude.

- Standards of work start to slip.

- Attendance pattern alters significantly.

- Dramatic changes in friendship groups.

Individually, these are not evidence of an issue, but you may wish to have a meeting with the learner if you become concerned about a mixture of changes. In terms of digital technology usage, you should look out for and possibly be suspicious if learners exhibit any of the signs above in combination with any of the following (based on signs described by Hinduja and Patchin, 2010: 3):

- Become obsessed and distracted with one or more social networks or messaging services.

- Isolate themselves from the physical world in favour of digital technologies. Conversely they may become suddenly very resistant to using digital technologies.

- Become very private or secretive about their digital technology usage.

- React uncharacteristically, or seemingly disproportionately when a new digital communication arrives.

If you do identify that cyberbullying is taking place, it is important that you support the learner through describing what has happened using a non-judgemental approach. Making them feel supported in this way will allow you to identify their issues and needs and progress towards a solution. Identifying and dealing with the perpetrator(s) is easier if they are other learners, but could be more difficult if they are external. If you are not able to deal with the situation in your institution you should seek the advice of your safeguarding officer who will be able to advise on the best course of action. If the learner is under 18 there may be grounds to treat the incident as a child protection issue if there is 'reasonable cause to suspect that a child... is suffering, or is likely to suffer significant harm' (Children Act, 1989) from the cyberbullying, which may be physical or mental. Even if the learner is over 18, you could still speak to the safeguarding officer, as outside agencies such as the police may wish to investigate and bring prosecution under the Malicious Communications Act 1988 or the Crime and Disorder Act 1998.

If you want to seek the advice of professionals from outside your organisation on digital safety and cyberbullying issues, making a call to the UK Safer Internet Centre (2015a) helpline could be a first step.

Example

Craig is occasionally teased about his weight by learners in your group, but he laughs this off and you have not been concerned until recently. After you met with Craig about his falling attendance, he confided in you that the comments he receives in class have started to annoy him a little, but more recently he has started to receive negative comments about his weight and looks on a popular photo-based social network. Twice these comments were accompanied by a threat of physical violence. The comments were from a profile using a pseudonym. Craig is sure that these comments must be coming from another learner in the class, as no one else comments on his weight. He is upset and worried.

Activity

Think about what you have learned so far and come up with a plan to help and support Craig to take steps to identify the perpetrators, stop the abuse and involve other professionals where appropriate.

If you or a colleague are cyberbullied

As a teacher or other member of staff, if you are cyberbullied by a learner, parent or other staff member, you should pursue the following steps, which are based upon advice issued by the University and College Union (no date) and the Department for Education (2014a, 2014b):

- **Do not respond to the cyberbullying or try to resolve it on your own.** Responding could make the situation worse and potentially lead to an escalation of the issue.

- **Report incidences of cyberbullying as you become aware of them.** Your line manager or a senior member of staff is usually the best person to speak to in the first instance. You may also wish to seek the advice of your union if you are a member of one. Don't wait to report something, the quicker it is reported, the quicker it can be dealt with.

- **Make sure the incident is investigated appropriately and help the investigation where possible.** A member of senior staff with responsibility for e-safety or health and safety is probably the most appropriate person to investigate. If you are able to collect evidence such as screenshots and downloads of the offending images and text then do so. If you are unable to do this, make the person investigating aware.

- **Make sure that the outcome resolves the issue and is satisfactory to you as the victim.** Your institution should follow their own procedures for dealing with such incidents, but if these procedures are inadequate, a union representative could help you to take the matter further. If your institution is unable to resolve the matter in-house, it may be time to seek external advice. In the first instance you could contact the UK Safer Internet Centre helpline (UK Safer Internet Centre, 2015a) and you may need to bring the matter to the attention of the police.

Digital safety issues relating to sexual exploitation

The most difficult digital safety issues to identify and resolve are those which happen mostly in private and have an element of control and embarrassment attached to them. Issues of sexual exploitation definitely fit within this category, but are some of the most dangerous and pernicious situations learners can find themselves in. As with cyberbullying, sexual exploitation through digital technologies is on the rise, with the Child Exploitation and Online Protection Centre, CEOP, receiving over 1000 reports of online child sexual abuse each year (CEOP, 2013: 6), which represents around 10 per cent of the estimated total number of children sexually abused in the UK each year. It is important to remember that the word *children* is used to mean anyone under the age of 18 and, even though the age of sexual consent is 16 in the UK, this does not mean that those aged between 16 and 18, and indeed those above 18 cannot be sexually abused and exploited. Therefore the issue is still one that the FE and Skills sector needs to address.

Grooming

The NSPCC (2015) defines grooming as being 'when someone builds an emotional connection with a child to gain their trust for the purposes of sexual abuse or exploitation'. In the FE and Skills sector, this definition can be expanded to cover vulnerable adults, as they may also be targets for grooming. According to NSPCC statistics (2015), victims are most likely to be targets for grooming and sexual abuse from people they know or are acquainted with. This could be anyone, from a family member, friend, professional, or someone who has gained their trust through communications in a digital environment.

The signs of a learner being the victim of grooming or having increased vulnerability to grooming could be multiple, but you should ask questions if any of the following become a problem:

- Sudden changes in behaviour, which could have the learner becoming secretive and not wishing to share details about their private life. They may also withdraw from friendships groups. Equally the learner may become boastful about a burgeoning relationship and wants to show off presents they have been promised or that have been purchased.

- Irrational behaviour, declining attendance and increasing risk-taking behaviour.

- Low self-esteem coupled with posting inappropriate photographs of themselves online. This may include posting semi-nude 'selfies' on social media.

- A change in the learner's use of aggressive or overly-sexualised language.

The signs of cyberbullying mentioned earlier could also be an indication of grooming taking place. If you suspect that a learner is being groomed, or is involved in grooming, you should contact your institution's safeguarding office as a matter of urgency so that immediate steps can be taken to stop abuse, support the victim and apprehend the perpetrator. It is important to remember that the fault always lies with the abuser, not the abused. Those being groomed should always be treated as a victim, regardless of how the grooming or abuse started.

Sexting

'Sexting', or cybersex as it is sometimes known, is the term given to using digital technologies to have conversations of a sexually explicit nature. Usually this involves sending a mixture of text or photo-based messages, but could also include participants sending sexually explicit short video clips of themselves or consist of live video chat. Usually, these communications are conducted privately by couples of a legally consenting age. But an NSPCC and Channel 4 News-conducted survey (Channel 4 News, 2012) suggests that, for teenagers, sexting is a normal and even expected part of relationships and friendships, with the sending and sharing of sexually explicit images not confined to adult relationships. This 'normality' could however lead to naivety, with sexting being used to lure young victims who's sexually explicit photos or videos are then shared for the purposes of bullying or grooming and sexual exploitation.

If you suspect that sexting is taking place for grooming and exploitation purposes, or if images and videos of under 18s are being shared through digital technologies you should report it to your institution's safeguarding office. The CEOP website (CEOP, no date), a command of the National Crime Agency, allows for the reporting of suspected child sexual abuse and exploitation online, and reports made to it are investigated by this special unit of the UK police force. If sexually explicit images of under 18s are shared between digital technologies then this could lead to a prosecution under child pornography laws.

Teachers in further education also have the legal powers to search learners, confiscate digital devices and erase photographs, images, recordings and other files which they deem inappropriate and believe may be used to cause 'serious harm'. This is set out under the 'Power of members of staff at further education institutions to search students', in Chapter 21, part 2 of the Education Act, 2011.

Grooming and sexting could take place through a number of different mediums and in a number of different ways. This could include through social media platforms, text messaging and, increasingly, through instant messaging apps, which have received media attention recently for their increase in usage and cases of children sharing inappropriate images of themselves and others through them.

Spotlight on ... instant messaging apps

These instant messaging apps have become extremely popular in the last few years and their growth has revolutionised the short message communications market, which was once dominated by SMS text messaging on mobile phones. Many learners may now use these apps as the primary route to communicate and connect with people.

The main advantages of instant messaging apps over SMS text messaging are:

- *Conversations can take place between two participants or between groups of multiple participants.*

- *Usually conversations in these apps work in a private manner, so that only invited participants can take part.*

- *Most instant messaging apps and services are free to use, with no costs regardless of the length of text or size of media being sent.*

- *They are not bound to one device and can be used across platforms. Therefore, a learner could start one conversation on a tablet PC or laptop at home, carry it on on their smartphone on the bus, and finish it on computer in college.*

These apps are very easy to download and start using, and the convenience of them combined with their abilities for sending media files and video chat makes them very useful digital communications tools. Snapchat and Kick are two instant messaging apps popular with young people and are not linked to other social networks. Facebook Messenger is linked to the users Facebook profile and friends list, and Google Hangouts, while being linked to the users Google account, is not so obviously part of a wider social network and has gained traction in being used by some organisations for work-based communications.

Online radicalisation and access to extremist material

As learners learn about how the world works and begin to explore and evolve their identity, they may become vulnerable to extremist political ideologies and religious views with hateful and destructive messages behind them. Websites, social network groups and videos can be found online which exist to promote such views and seek to 'radicalise' young and vulnerable people to join extremist groups and spread their messages. In some extreme cases, this could lead to terrorist acts being committed.

Very often the person becoming radicalised can start with grievances towards, or dissatisfaction with, 'the system' and may feel that they have no place or purpose in society because of unemployment or perceived injustices. As teachers in the FE and Skills sector, we regularly encounter learners who fit this description and very often success stories occur where we help learners to turn their lives around, gain good skilled jobs, see a positive way forward for their lives and are able to engage with mainstream democracy to affect change. However, teachers must be aware that extremist content is readily available for those who may want to access it, or encourage others to access it.

The new Counter-terrorism and Security Act 2015 requires FE and Skills sector teachers and institutions to stop such content being accessed, used and disseminated within their institution, and to safeguard against extremism. The safeguarding role this legislation imposes is called the 'prevent' duty. The Education and Training Foundation (ETF) has setup a dedicated website that provides guidance on the new legislation for the FE and Skills sector and gives specific advice on the prevent duty (ETF, 2015). As this legislation and the policy around it were being introduced as this book went to press, it is likely that the exact nature of the effect on the FE and Skills sector, as well as the methods for implementation, will be become more clear later in 2015 and in 2016.

Your IT network department should have produced an institution-wide 'acceptable usage of the network and IT equipment' policy which may explicitly mention such activities. This legislation places specific duties on to the FE and Skills sector to introduce levels of Internet filtering which block extremist content and to have an Internet safety policy which covers extremism (Cook, 2015).

Professional conduct in digital environments

In Chapter 7 we looked at how you can manage your digital profiles and identity. Through this the idea of having separate 'professional' and 'personal' identities was discussed, with the author making the case for the view that it may not be appropriate to try to form two separate identities, but instead keep a balance between the two and present one voice which is your own. However, this does not mean that you should make all your social networks open and accept everyone as friends. Instead you can use different digital environments for different purposes, with somewhere like Facebook being your 'close friends and family space', while Twitter is a 'work and learning space'. With this approach and your own digital safety needs in mind, the following are tips on how to remain professional in digital environments and interact with learners:

- **Only use communication channels provided by your institution to communicate with learners**. This includes your work email account and the virtual learning environment, VLE. Do not add learners or their families as friends on social networks you see as friends and family spaces. Check to see if your institution has a staff usage of social media policy.

- **Think about the language you use in digital communications with learners**. Stick to the facts and be unambiguous, be professional, and do not saying anything which could be misconstrued as flirtatious, risky or offensive.

- **If you know a learner outside college and are friends with them online, declare it**. Tell your line manager the exact nature of the relationship and agree to a way forward for the separation of personal and professional communications while this person is a learner. Your institution may make reference to this in their social media policy.

Digital data security

The protection and security of personal data and information are a key responsibility for professionals working in education institutions. At any one time, you may have access to or responsibility for the following data held digitally by your institution:

- **Your own network account/login details**. This gives access to your email account, network drives and files, the VLE and a range of other systems and resources. Account login details will usually consist of a username and password. Requirements for strong passwords have become more stringent in recent years, with set lengths and requirements for combinations of upper and lowercase letters and the use of one or more number. This is due to longer and more complex passwords being more difficult to hack or guess.

- **Confidential details about learners**. This could include details such as their home address, their age, grades and achievements, criminal records, health, and benefits status. These could be held in a variety of systems and files, such as learner management and data systems, and reports to qualification bodies.

- **Human resources systems and records**. If you line manage someone within your institution you may have access to their confidential employment details through an online system.

- **Learning resource packages, information resources and confidential assessments**. Your institution is likely to subscribe to or have purchased licences for a range of learning resource packages and information systems, such as digital content and activities which can be used in class, and collections of e-books, articles and other information resources. These will all be subject to a licence stipulating how they can be used and by whom. You may also have access to systems controlling assessments and examinations, which need to be kept controlled and locked down, perhaps to a group of specific persons.

In order to fulfil your responsibilities for keeping safe all the sensitive data you have access to and may have responsibility for managing, you should consider doing the following:

- **Only access the most sensitive of data on equipment provided by your institution**. This stops potential saving of passwords by Web browsers and accidental or purposeful access by other users of the machine. If you do have to use a non-work PC to access your accounts, make sure you clear your browsing history, saved passwords and cached content in the browser's settings.

- **Set the strongest passwords possible for work-based accounts** and choose different passwords from those you use for personal, non-work accounts.

- **Never (ever!) share your password** or let anyone else use a machine logged on as you.

- **Make sure you have the latest software updates** for your operating system, browser, virus and security software and other software you use.

- **Avoid accessing insecure and untrusted websites** on equipment you use to access work-based accounts. Insecure websites are usually monitored and tracked by security software which will warn you if there might be phishing scams and potential viruses hiding within the sites, which could 'mine' data such as account login details.

- **Evaluate and assess digital technologies for safety and security before you use them to store confidential and sensitive data**. See Chapter 5 for more information on this.

Activity

Take a look at the UK government's Cyber Streetwise website (HM Government, 2015) to read their advice on digital security. What steps can you take to protect your own and others' digital data both at home and at work? Is there anything which you currently do not do which is leaving you unprotected?

Activity

Think creatively about the issues raised in this chapter. How can you use your knowledge and skills to help raise awareness of digital safety and security issues across your institution and encourage learners and staff to become good digital citizens? Think about activities you could work with colleagues and learners on. Why not try some of the following?

- *Run a digital campaign to raise awareness.*

- *Design and deliver a lesson using digital tools for activities.*

- *Organise events and activities for the annual Safer Internet Day (UK Safer Internet Centre, 2015b).*

Activity

Think critically about the principle of 'openness' and the drives to create a more open and accessible Internet, and its relationship to digital safety and security. Are the two compatible and, if so, how? Think about how you can understand and promote both in balance within your work in the FE and Skills sector.

Summary

In this chapter you have learned:

- About the concept of digital citizenship and the rights and responsibilities we have in digital environments.

- What your legal, ethical and professional duties are in relation to digital safety and digital security

- About cyberbullying, grooming and pressurisation online, and how to recognise and respond to them.

- How to manage your communications with learners in digital environments and professional conduct.

- About digital data, and how to keep it safe and secure.

References and further reading

AoC, ACM, ATL, GMB, Unite, Unison and UCU (2008) *Joint Agreement on Guidance for Harassment and Bullying in Employment in Further Education Colleges*. Available at: https://www.atl.org.uk/Images/Agreement%20on%20harassment%20%26%20bullying%20in%20FE.pdf.

CEOP (2013) *Threat Assessment of Child Sexual Exploitation and Abuse*. Available at: http://www.ceop.police.uk/Documents/ceopdocs/CEOP_TACSEA2013_240613%20FINAL.pdf.

CEOP (no date) Available at: http://www.ceop.police.uk/.

Channel 4 News (2012) 'Generation sex: explicit pics "the norm" for teens.' Available at: http://www.channel4.com/news/generation-sex-explicit-pics-the-norm-for-teens.

ChildLine (2013) 'Can I tell you something?', *ChildLine Review*, 2012/13. Available at: http://www.nspcc.org.uk/globalassets/documents/research-reports/childline-review-2012-2013.pdf.

Children Act (1989) Available at: http://www.legislation.gov.uk/ukpga/1989/41/contents.

Cook, A (2015) 'New counter-terrorism duties: what schools need to know', *Guardian*, 2 March. Available at: http://www.theguardian.com/teacher-network/2015/mar/02/counter-terrorism-duties-schools-need-to-know.

Crime and Disorder Act (1998) Available at: http://www.legislation.gov.uk/ukpga/1998/37/contents.

DCSF and DIUS (2009) *Safe from Bullying in Further Education Colleges*. Available at: http://www.anti-bullyingalliance.org.uk/media/7488/safe_from_bullying-fe.pdf.

DfE (2014a) *Cyberbullying: Advice for Headteachers and School Staff*. Available at: https://www.gov.uk/government/uploads/system/uploads/attachment_data/file/374850/Cyberbullying_Advice_for_Headteachers_and_School_Staff_121114.pdf.

DfE (2014b) *Preventing and Tackling Bullying: Advice for Headteachers, Staff and Governing Bodies*. Available at: https://www.gov.uk/government/uploads/system/uploads/attachment_data/file/409061/preventing_and_tackling_bullying_october2014.pdf.

DfE (2015) *Keeping Children Safe in Education: Statutory Guidance for Schools and Colleges*. Available at: https://www.gov.uk/government/uploads/system/uploads/attachment_data/file/418686/Keeping_children_safe_in_education.pdf.

Ditch the Label (2015) *The Wireless Report 2015*. Available at: http://www.ditchthelabel.org/the-wireless-report-2014/.

Education Act (2011, c. 21) Available at: http://www.legislation.gov.uk/ukpga/2011/21/pdfs/ukpga_20110021_en.pdf.

Equality Act (2010) Available at: http://www.legislation.gov.uk/ukpga/2010/15/contents.

ETF (2015) *Prevent for Further Education and Training*. Available at: http://www.preventforfeandtraining.org.uk/.

Hinduja, S and Patchin, J W (2010) *Cyberbullying: Identification, Prevention, and Response*. Available at: http://svrcindustries.com/download/cyberbullying_identification_prevention_response_fact_sheet.pdf.

HM Government (2015) *Cyber Streetwise*. Available at: https://www.cyberstreetwise.com/.

Hoechsmann, M and Poyntz, S R (2012) *Media Literacies: A Critical Introduction*. Oxford: Wiley-Blackwell.

Malicious Communications Act (1988) Available at: http://www.legislation.gov.uk/ukpga/1988/27/contents.

NASUWT (2015) *Huge Rise in Teachers being Abused on Social Media*. Available at: http://www.nasuwt.org.uk/Whatsnew/NASUWTNews/PressReleases/NASUWT_013930.

NSPCC (2015) *Grooming.* Available at: http://www.nspcc.org.uk/preventing-abuse/child-abuse-and-neglect/grooming/.

Poore, M (2013) *Using Social Media in the Classroom: A Best Practice Guide.* London: Sage.

UK Safer Internet Centre (2015a) 'Helpline.' Available at: http://www.saferinternet.org.uk/about/helpline.

UK Safer Internet Centre (2015b) *Safer Internet Day.* http://www.saferinternet.org.uk/safer-internet-day.

University and College Union (no date) *Practical Steps to Ensure Internet Safety.* Available at: https://www.ucu.org.uk/media/pdf/o/9/hsfacts_internetsafety.pdf.

White, D S and LeCornu, A (2011) 'Visitors and residents: a new typology for online engagement', *First Monday*, 16 (9). Available at: http://firstmonday.org/ojs/index.php/fm/article/view/3171/3049#p4.

White, J P (2013) 'In the news #1: trolls, abuse, threats and cyberbullying', *Teach Digital Literacy* blog, 11 August. Available at: http://teachdigitalliteracy.com/2013/08/11/in-the-news-1/.

Willard, N (2012) *Cyber Savvy: Embracing Digital Safety and Civility.* Thousand Oaks, CA: Sage.

In this chapter you will learn:

- What copyright and licensing are and how they relate to digital content.
- How digital content may be used for educational purposes under UK copyright legislation.
- About the different types of licences FE and Skills sector institutions need to purchase in order to use digital content.
- To think about how we teach about rights and responsibilities with digital content and tackle plagiarism.
- About choosing licences and ensuring copyright compliance when publishing your own digital content.

Links to the Digitally Literate FE and Skills Teacher Framework

6.   *Understands and leads on digital safety, responsibility and citizenship.*

6.2   *Understands own legal, ethical and professional rights and responsibilities when using, creating and publishing digital content.*

6.3   *Understands the definition of digital citizenship and recognises the rights and responsibilities we each have in digital environments.*

As with the previous chapter, this chapter covers legal, ethical and moral issues the FE and Skills teacher is likely to face in their professional use of digital technologies. The information given in this chapter is intended to stimulate critical thinking around the issues and to encourage ways that you can increase your digital creativity, while remaining compliant with legal and professional duties. As is stated at the beginning of the previous chapter, this is not intended to be detailed legal advice and guidance. References to sources of legal advice and guidance will be referenced throughout.

What are the legal issues around digital content?

All published content, whether in print or in a digital form, has an owner. This is usually the person or persons who created/authored the content, but it could also be an organisation that commissioned the content to be created and published. Owners of content have legal rights over their works, which includes the right to be acknowledged as the author of the content when it is reused, and have the right to decide and stipulate conditions on how, when and for what purposes their works may be reused, copied, edited/re-packaged, displayed/performed/shown, stored and distributed. These rights are commonly known as copyright, and the associated conditions a copyright holder may decide on and stipulate are usually managed by licensing the content.

Rights and licensing are extremely important concepts for FE and Skills practitioners then, as much of our work involves using digital content in a wide variety of ways. This can include everything from playing a video clip to a class of students, to reusing a resource you found online. You may also be publishing your own work online in the form of a blog, or sharing your teaching resources, and doing this would also require a thought for who owns the copyright to these works and the licensing of them. In this chapter, all these ways in which we use and publish digital content will be explored, as will others.

Freely available = free to reuse?

As much digital content is free to access and view online, it is a common misconception that it is therefore freely available to be reused by anyone, and is exempt from copyright and licensing. All digital content is still copyrighted to an owner, and that owner will have conditions on how it can be reused, whether it is free to access or requires payment to access. Therefore, you should always look for details of the content owner and a licence/conditions of usage statement before reusing it in your work.

Most owners of freely available digital content will have published it with the express intention that it is consumed in some may, but you should think about the following when looking for rights holder and licence details:

- **Who has published it/where have you found it?** Very often digital content is not found in the place where it was originally published. This happens frequently with the sharing of content. Social media websites, such as YouTube and Vimeo, sometimes contain videos uploaded and posted by an account which is not that of the copyright holder. This may in itself be breaking the terms of the content's licence and may have been done without the copyright holder's knowledge and permission. As a rule, only use digital content from the original source – i.e. the website or social media account of the author or publisher.

- **Both organisations and people can be authors and publishers.** This has been stated a number of times in this book, but it is worth reiterating, as it is often questioned. In the digital age, anyone can publish content they have authored online, thereby making them the copyright holder, and both author and publisher. Conversely, organisations are able to have content authored on their behalf, to which they own the copyright. They then become both author and publisher. Therefore, you should look for clues as to who the author and publisher are. Chapter 6 lists these criteria in the section on evaluating digital resources.

- **Copyright does not have to be 'registered'.** The combined acts of authoring content and publishing it (making it available) are enough to establish the copyright on an item.

No system of copyright registration exists, and owners do not have to display a notice, or the copyright symbol, ©, stating whom the content is copyrighted to – although it helps users greatly if they do!

- **'Free' content may be limited by licence.** Sometimes, freely available digital content is only available to access for a limited period of time or set number of times before payment has to be made, or before it expires and is no longer available online. This is particularly true of catch-up and on-demand TV services. For example, the availability of content on the BBC iPlayer is time limited, in most cases, to thirty days after the original broadcast (BBC, 2015). This could be problematic if you are instructing learners to watch the video as a part of homework, or are embedding it into the virtual learning environment (VLE). The terms of the licence may also stipulate that advertisements are displayed within the content, that sponsorship messages appear, or that users create an account and login before being able to access digital content. You may want to check for such conditions and their exact nature before instructing learners to access a resource.

Activity

Investigate the copyright holders and licences for the digital content you use with learners.

- *Are you using video clips, articles, images and other information and media from the original source?*

- *For any content where the source is unclear or is obviously not the original one, look for details of authors and publishers. Using this information, can you track down the original source of the material?*

Using digital content for educational purposes

The Copyright Designs and Patents Act 1988, and its various amendments, gives copyright owners the mechanisms to receive an income from reuse of their work through the use of licences which organisations have to purchase. This includes education institutions, such as further education colleges, which have long been able to purchase licences enabling them to use more traditional resources in an education context. However, this legislation was passed long before the wide range of digital content existed and learning technologies such as VLEs and interactive whiteboards (IWBs) were available for teachers to use. As such, the showing of certain types of content on IWBs, the sharing of it on VLEs and the copying, editing and distribution of it was not covered by the legislation, even for educational purposes.

To rectify this situation the UK government amended the Copyright Designs and Patents Act 1988 in 2014 to extend and clarify the rights of those working in the education sectors and for learners, students and researchers to use copyrighted digital content. For those working in the FE and Skills sector, the new regulations for both the education sectors and for those working with disabled people are of particular importance (Copyright and Rights in Performances (Research, Education, Libraries and Archives) Regulations, 2014; Copyright and Rights in Performances (Disability) Regulations, 2014). For a full list of the benefits these changes have given to education professionals and learners, the Intellectual Property Office (2014a; 2014b; 2014c) have produced two documents and a website which give the details. The following, taken from the guidance by the Intellectual Property Office, are the two main amendments for those working in the FE and Skills sector:

- **Education professionals can make copies of copyrighted works, regardless of format, and distribute them to/share them with learners, as long as they have the correct licences to do so.** This means that, in addition to portions of text-based content being copiable and distributable, now video and audio clips, image-based content and any other media can also be copied/shared and distributed via VLEs to learners or shown on IWBs in the classroom. There are conditions attached to this usage though, the main being the concept of 'fair dealing'. This legal term is used to mean that only a fair and reasonable amount of any content may be used to illustrate a point or add to the learning of a concept, and the author, publisher and/or source of the content must be acknowledged. Therefore you should only share the most relevant clip of a film or piece of audio. This is so that reuse of these materials for educational purposes does not affect sales of commercially available content and resources. For details of the amounts you can copy from books and of using broadcast television recordings and catch-up/on-demand services in your teaching, see the information on licences below.

- **Copyrighted works, regardless of format, can be transferred into accessible versions for learners with disabilities, as long as the accessible version is not already available commercially.** This means that educational institutions can legally change the format of or edit any print, text-based, video or audio content based on the needs of a disabled learner. This could include printing text-based resources into braille, creating audio versions, making large-print copies available or changing the font type, size and colour; and creating and adding subtitles and audio-description to video and audio content. It is worth noting that this is not always necessary, as very often adaptive software is available to do some of this. This includes screen readers and magnifiers, and many e-book reading platforms have a range of tools for visual and hearing impaired users. If such tools are owned by your institution, or if the publisher sells a version of the content with these features built in, then the copyright legislation would require that those alternatives are used rather than something being created in-house.

Licences required to use digital content

As was mentioned earlier, UK legislation allows for a range of licensing organisations to exist which collect a fee from organisations for the reuse of copyrighted materials. Even though UK copyright legislation now covers education professionals to reuse copyrighted content in a range of ways for non-commercial educational purposes, institutions are required by the same laws to purchase and hold licences before they can use content. Various licences exist which cover most activities FE and Skills sector institutions undertake. The following are the three main licences all FE and Skills sector institutions need in order to cover the main educational activities undertaken with digital technologies:

- **The Copyright Licensing Agency (CLA) licence** – this licence allows for copies to be made from books, journals and magazines (both from print and digital copies), as well as from some websites and other digital resources. These can then be shown on IWBs or distributed via VLEs for the purpose of being learning resources. This includes text-based content, images, charts, diagrams and illustrations. There is a limit to the amount of content which may be copied under the licence and that is a maximum of five per cent of the total content from the resource or one article or chapter. You can find out more about the CLA licence, what it covers and what it does not cover on the CLA's website for the FE and Skills sector (CLA, 2015a).

- **The Educational Recording Agency (ERA) licence and TV licence** – for live television broadcasts to be legally received and watched within FE and Skills sector institutions, a TV licence must be purchased by the institution. This includes the watching of live television broadcasts through the Internet (sometime known as TV over IP, in which IP stands for Internet Protocol). If you want to make recordings of television broadcasts, either to DVD or on to your institution's network and then show them in class or put them on to your VLE for learners to access, your institution will need to purchase the ERA licence. The ERA licence also covers you to show televisions programmes from catch-up and on-demand services and for learners to watch them within the institution. The ERA licence only covers UK terrestrial broadcasts though, so subscription television services and channels not broadcast in the UK are not covered. You can find out more information about the ERA licence and if your institution has purchased it on the ERA website (ERA, 2015).

- **The Newspaper Licensing Agency (NLA) licence** – the NLA licence allows UK newspapers, both in their print and digital versions, to be used as education resources. This includes making 'cuttings' of articles and distributing these to learners, although not all newspapers allow for cuttings to be distributed digitally. The CLA has been appointed to administer the NLA licence for education institutions and more details can be found on the CLA's website (CLA, 2015c).

Unfortunately, there is no one licensing agency for other types of digital content and learning resources, such as software, apps and information resources like e-books. Individual licences will come with each resource your institution purchases. Usually, a specific education or institution-wide licence will need to be purchased. If you are using any digital tools, such as cloud-based software and apps in your practice, speak to your IT team to find out if a licence is required.

A lot of freely accessible digital content and tools is now issued with a licence from a licence provider, which gives a clear and simple list of the do's and don'ts of using the content/resource. The most common of these is the Creative Commons (CC) licence scheme which allows content creators and publishers to pick from a set range of licences and attach them to their content. The CC badge is then visible on the content for users to click and find out how they can reuse the content and for what purposes. How CC licences work and can be used is explore later in this chapter. Another scheme in use is the Collective Licensing Scheme, which is identified by 'What can I do with this content?' This scheme is primarily aimed at publishers who are members of the CLA's Collective Licensing Scheme, and it allows them to pick licence terms and apply a badge to their digital content. More information on this scheme can be found on their website (CLA, no date).

Freely available digital content from the UK government, related departments and some other agencies and public bodies is covered by the Open Government Licence. This is administered by the National Archives (no date). Types of digital content covered by this include the content of government websites, statistics, policy documents, open data sets and legislation. It now also includes the reuse of freely available Ordnance Survey map data, which previously required a separate licence to be purchased by education institutions (Ordnance Survey, 2015).

Your institution will need to obtain other licences if it wishes to use the growing range of digital content for purposes other than those directly related to learning and teaching. This may include showing films and other videos for entertainment or paid performance purposes, or streaming music for public consumption. This could potentially affect commercial training areas within your institution, such as salons and cafes. Ask your learning resource centre or IT team for advice on the licences required.

Activity

Think about your subject specialism and the teaching team you work as part of:

- *Do you think that the rights and responsibilities around copyright and licensing are understood by the team?*

- *What are the most important points relevant to you and your immediate colleagues?*

- *If more of one type of digital content/resource and method of reusing it is particularly relevant to your subject area and the way you teach it, try putting together a poster which lists the do's and don'ts of this practice that you could use with colleagues.*

- *If you require further information and advice look on the Copyright User website (2015), which gives independent advice for both creators and users across a wide range of purposes.*

Publishing and licensing your own content

In Chapters 4, 5 and 7 we looked at the process of being creative with digital technologies and showcasing your knowledge, skills, talents and abilities through the creation and publication of digital content online. It is important when doing this that you consider the copyright implications and any licences you should attach. This should not be seen as a restriction to your creativity but an important step that will:

- Give legal protection to your digital content against misuse.

- Allow you to check who owns your content, to protect you from legal claims.

- Give a more of a professional feel to your content and get it noticed.

- Ensure correct acknowledgement is given to your work by those reusing it.

- State clearly how you wish your content to be used by others.

The first step is to ensure that you are the copyright holder of your digital content and have the right to publish it online. In most cases you will be the holder if you are the sole creator of the digital content. However, you may need to check the licensing of any third-party content, such as audio and video clips, as you may not be able to re-publish these. You also need to be clear on where you created the content and for what purpose. If you created the content in your own time and it was not specifically done in pursuit of your job role, then you should be able to publish it as your work. However, some employers may want to be credited as the or an author if the content was created for use in your job, on the institution's equipment or during your working hours. Check if your institution has a specific policy on intellectual property.

When you have established who the copyright holder is and have their permission to publish, you need to consider where you will publish your content and how to promote it. Various different ways of doing this are explored in Chapter 7. The next consideration is how to label your content with a copyright notice and make your intentions for how it is to be reused clear with a licence.

The most clear way to make the copyright notice obvious is to insert your name, or that of the copyright holder if not you, with the copyright symbol © and the year. This allows those reusing it to easily acknowledge who the author/creator is.

The easiest way to licence your content for reuse is to use a Creative Commons (CC) licence. These are easy to generate and give you a range of options that will be presented to potential users when they click the CC badge next to your digital content. To generate a CC badge to cover all content on your website or to accompany specific digital content, follow the easy-to-use instructions on the CC website (Creative Commons, no date b). It is also a good idea to read the CC Wiki page on considerations to make before licensing before you begin ('Considerations for licensors and licensees', 2013). As the licences undergo regular updates you should consult the CC website for details of the latest licence types available (Creative Commons, no date a). Once you have selected a licence the CC website will generate a piece of HTML script that, when put into the HTML of your website, will display a badge with the licence details. If you are using a website design tool or software, there may be a tool built in to embed objects and media. This will allow you to paste in the HTML script for the badge.

Example

Suzie has her own website on which she blogs about working in the theatre industry and teaching BTEC performing arts, as well as uploading related photos she takes and video clips. Due to working in the theatre industry for many years, she has a basic understanding of how copyright works, and has always sought the permission of the rights holders before filming performances and making them available online. Suzie uses CC licensing for most of

(Continued)

(Continued)

the content she uploads online and uses the latest version of the 'Attribution-ShareAlike' licence. This licence allows others to edit, adapt, republish and share her work, as long as they acknowledge her original source.

For most pieces, she also allows commercial reuse, as this may lead to even more exposure for her content. Suzie's website attracts a lot of traffic and has received acknowledgement from industry professionals in the past. Therefore, she decided that showcasing the theatrical work of her learners on her website, through photographs of the set design work they had done, would give them a confidence boost and may even lead to opportunities for them. She discusses this with the learners who are happy for this to happen and for full credit to be given to them on the website. Suzie is concerned though about whether this is permitted by college policy and decides to ask her line manager. The manager likes the idea in principle, but makes enquiries into whether this is permitted. It is realised that the college does not have a specific policy covering this, but the Senior Management Team ask that the name of the college be acknowledged in the material and that commercial reuse not be allowed in the licence for this content. Suzie follows the advice and proceeds, feeling more confident about the project and pleased that she checked before going ahead.

Understanding and reducing plagiarism

In Chapter 8 the idea of digital rights and responsibilities was explored in the context of digital citizenship, and the idea of being ethical in our approach to digital technology usage was a key part of this. In Chapter 6, ethical use of information and media was also discussed as being a key strand of being information literate. Ethical usage of digital technologies, and our understanding of the relationship between them and our critical thought process and creativity, is a key element of digital literacy then. So, in becoming digitally literate we must learn to respect the rights and conditions of content owners and accept the responsibilities that come with them. This is in addition to understanding our own rights regarding content we create and publish.

The concept of plagiarism is well suited to understanding and thinking around the ethical dilemmas that occur around these issues. As well as being grounded in the technical aspects of copyright law, licensing, citation and referencing, it also challenges us to think about what 'content' and 'products' are, especially as plagiarism covers the concept of stealing ideas, whereas in copyright law, ideas cannot be copyrighted.

If done well then, teaching about plagiarism can lead to some extremely interesting conversations with learners and can generate lots of critical thought. When this is then used to lead into research or content creation-based activities, learners tend to engage at a deeper level and are guided by different principles. This in turn can cut down on the amount of mindless cutting and pasting that can occur, as learner start to see a reason to cite sources and reference correctly. Try these approaches with learners to get them critically thinking about using digital content ethically and acknowledging sources:

- **Start with the ethics and critical thinking, leave the mechanistic approaches to later** – teaching the mechanics of citation and referencing in isolation will not help learners to see the relevance of it and could seem abstract without an understanding of why it is important. Use active learning around plagiarism to make them understand why acknowledging sources is important.

- **Make it real, make it active** – use real-life and relevant examples of plagiarism as discussion points, and put the learners in the hot seat by developing role play activities where they are the individual who has had plagiarism committed against them. This active learning approach will allow them to gain a deep understanding of the issues. For some real-life plagiarism examples, covering the music industry, video games and other media, take a look at the regularly updated Wikipedia page on the subject ('List of plagiarism incidents', 2015).

- **Give them the right 'tools', at the right level** – FE and Skills learners could be on courses at a wide range of levels, and may all have different destinations in mind. Therefore, academic referencing styles, such as Harvard and MLA may not be the most suitable way of teaching learners how to acknowledge sources of information and ideas. Instead you could first approach this by teaching them to acknowledge authors, dates and URLS in their work, without worrying too much about exact punctuation. This can then build to incorporate other elements over time. Very often, learners' reluctance to reference is due to concern that they can't remember exactly how to do it, and are afraid of getting it wrong.

If you do need to teach copyright as part of your curriculum, or if knowledge of it will be useful to learners in their future careers, take a look at the resources on the CLA's website on copyright for a range of FE subjects (CLA, 2015b), and two good downloadable activities on teaching copyright from Jorum which were originally designed to be used for staff training events, but could be easily adapted for use with learners (Moore, 2014; Morrison et al., 2015).

Summary

In this chapter you have learned:

- What copyright and licensing are and how they relate to digital content.

- How digital content may be used for educational purposes under UK copyright legislation.

- About the different types of licences FE and Skills sector institutions need to purchase in order to use digital content.

- To think about how we teach about rights and responsibilities with digital content and tackle plagiarism.

- About choosing licences and ensuring copyright compliance when publishing your own digital content.

References and further reading

BBC (2015) BBC iPlayer – programmes – availability. Available at: http://iplayerhelp.external.bbc.co.uk/tv/progs_avail.

CLA (2015a) *The Copyright Licensing Agency – Further Education*. Available at: http://fe.cla.co.uk/.

CLA (2015b) *Copyright on your Course*. Available at: http://fe.cla.co.uk/copyright-related-resources/copyright-in-further-education-courses/.

CLA (2015c) *NLA Education Establishment Licence*. Available at: http://fe.cla.co.uk/your-fe-licence/nla-education-establishment-licence/.

CLA (no date) *What Can I do with this Content?* Available at: http://whatcanidowiththiscontent.com/.

'Considerations for licensors and licensees' (2013). Available at: https://wiki.creativecommons.org/Considerations_for_licensors_and_licensees.

Copyright and Rights in Performances (Disability) Regulations 2014 (SI 2014/1384) Available at: http://www.legislation.gov.uk/uksi/2014/1384/contents/made.

Copyright and Rights in Performances (Research, Education, Libraries and Archives) Regulations 2014 (SI 2014/1372) Available at: http://www.legislation.gov.uk/uksi/2014/1372/contents/made.

Copyright Designs and Patents Act (1988) Available at: https://www.gov.uk/government/uploads/system/uploads/attachment_data/file/382206/Copyright_Designs_and_Patents_Act_1988.pdf.

Copyright User (2015) Copyright User website. Available at: www.copyrightuser.org.

Creative Commons (no date a) *About the Licenses*. Available at: http://creativecommons.org/licenses/.

Creative Commons (no date b) *Choose a Licence*. Available at: http://creativecommons.org/choose/.

ERA (2015) *The Educational Recording Agency*. Available at: http://www.era.org.uk/.

Hoechsmann, M and Poyntz, S R (2012) *Media Literacies: A Critical Introduction*. Chichester: Blackwell Publishing.

Intellectual Property Office (2014a) *Exceptions to Copyright: Education and Teaching*. Available at: https://www.gov.uk/government/uploads/system/uploads/attachment_data/file/375951/Education_and_Teaching.pdf.

Intellectual Property Office (2014b) *Exceptions to Copyright: Accessible Formats for Disabled People*. Available at: https://www.gov.uk/government/uploads/system/uploads/attachment_data/file/375952/Accessible_formats_for_disabled_people.pdf.

Intellectual Property Office (2014c) *Intellectual Property – Guidance: Exceptions to Copyright*. Available at: https://www.gov.uk/exceptions-to-copyright.

'List of plagiarism incidents' (2015) Available at: http://en.wikipedia.org/wiki/List_of_plagiarism_incidents.

Moore, A (2014) 'Can I copy? A snakes and ladders game for copyright do's and don'ts.' Available at: http://find.jorum.ac.uk/resources/19277.

Morrison, C, Korn, N and Secker, J (2015) *Copyright the Card Game*. Available at: http://find.jorum.ac.uk/resources/19369.

National Archives (no date) *Licensing for Reuse*. Available at: http://www.nationalarchives.gov.uk/information-management/re-using-public-sector-information/licensing-for-re-use/.

Ordnance Survey (2015) *Licensed Use of Ordnance Survey Data by Educational and Teacher Training Establishments*. Available at: http://www.ordnancesurvey.co.uk/education-research/maps-for-schools/copyright.html.

10 FUTURE DEVELOPMENT PLANNING

In this chapter you will learn:

- About undertaking skills development and the metacognitive process.
- About reflecting upon your digital literacy development and methods for doing so.
- How to action plan for the next step in your digital literacy development.
- How to monitor and use future trends.

Links to the Digitally Literate FE and Skills Teacher Framework

7. *Plans for continuous professional development (CPD) and tracks digital trends. Makes use of digital tools for reflection.*

1. *Understands their own position as a digitally literate professional and the relationship between skills and practice.*

1.1 *Understands their own digital needs, abilities and practice, and plans for their own development.*

Undertaking your own digital literacy skills development

Throughout the chapters of this book we have explored how teachers in the FE and Skills sector can improve their digital literacy by developing their knowledge and skills in digital technologies and their practice with them. The key elements and principles of being a digitally literate person, such as being a critical thinker and understanding personal creativity, have been reiterated in a number of places, and this has hopefully led to a development in your thinking around the subjects and your confidence within them. Development as a digitally literate person does not end with this book though, as digital technologies, the FE and Skills sector, and the digital skills we require as educational professionals will always continue to evolve. As the Jisc definition of digital literacy from Chapter 2 states, 'What it means to be digitally literate changes over time and across contexts' (Jisc, 2014). As with digital literacy skills themselves then, remaining engaged in the development of personal and professional digital literacy can only be achieved by being critical and by nurturing our creativity.

To take responsibility for the process of your own digital literacy skills development, recognising your current knowledge and skills, and understand the right strategy by which to improve them, is a metacognitive approach, as defined by Flavell (1979), and expanded upon by Schraw (1998) and Hartman (1998). Applying their metacognitive approach to digital literacy development enables us to consider and use the following processes:

- **Identify our own abilities, strengths and weaknesses in a particular area** – this involves looking at current practices with digital technologies, as well as skills and abilities in using and applying them, and identifying what you need to do in order to improve or change.

- **Understand the knowledge and skills required to become literate in a particular area and form a strategy to achieve it** – the digitally literate teacher framework allows you to identify what is required. Working through the chapters can form part of your strategy for gaining it.

- **Self-regulate and control our own learning and development of digital literacy** – through self-monitoring and evaluation of our digital practice we can check that we are applying critical thought and creativity to our use of digital technologies, are continuously developing our skills and checking our ability, and are monitoring best practice to inform and improve our own digital practice. To go further in this and really take ownership of your own development will require going beyond the digitally literate teacher framework; adding skills relevant to your subject area, curriculum and practice out in industry to it; and identifying the key parts of these skills and action planning the next steps.

Activity

Consider the last point above.

- *What else do you need to do with digital technologies that is not covered in this book or by the digitally literate teacher framework?*

- *What other strands of knowledge and skills can you add to the framework?*

Reflecting and action planning using digital tools

In Chapter 5, selecting and using digital tools for productivity was discussed. The variety in the types of digital tools listed, including cloud-based storage services and tools such as word processors, note-taking software, voice note and video-recording apps, allow us to carry out the tasks we have always had to carry out, but in new ways. Digital tools also allow us, though to do things that we weren't previously able to do before apps, cloud-based tools and mobile devices existed. If utilised correctly then, the application of digital tools to continuous professional development activities could be transformational.

Reflection and action planning in particular stand out as being practices where digital tools enable us to carry out tasks, but also find new ways of recording what we do. The following are elements of reflection to which tools can be utilised:

- **Recording instant thoughts and feelings** – if you carry a smartphone or a tablet PC, there is a wide range of apps you could use to capture your responses to situations, experiences. If you need to write something down, then note-taking apps could be particularly useful. If you need to capture your emotional responses, as well as the words, using voice and video-recording apps could be extremely useful. The front-facing camera, sometimes now referred to as the 'selfie cam', on phones and tablets is ideal for capturing these moments in time. You can then analyse these when reflecting later.

- **Filling in reflection journals and action plans** – you, or your institution, may have set models of reflection or particular forms and writing frames. Largely these will be paper based, but in this format they can become difficult to carry around. Therefore it may be useful to choose a cloud-based service and app on which to store your reflective journal templates. That way you can edit them on the go while still keeping them saved in one location – see the CPD section on the author's website for a list of links to reflective journal documents, and the latest version of my action-planning tool (White, 2015). The Society for Education and Training (SET) have an online CPD tool for members, which could be used as a part of the CPD needs assessment, reflection and action-planning process (Society for Education and Training, 2015).

In developing digital literacy, professionals will have many different types of experiences and applications for the skills. Therefore, your reflection will not just be on utilising digital technologies and skills for learning and teaching, although that will form a large part of it – you should also reflect on the other parts of your professional practice where you utilise digital technologies, critically and creatively engage with them, and learn new knowledge, skills and methods of practice.

Activity

Create three sets of reflective questions for your experiences of digital technologies and skills:

- *A set for your learning and teaching experiences.*
- *A set for development of your specialist subject knowledge.*
- *A set for other work activities, such as administrative, management or research activities.*

Think about the reflective questions you need to ask in each. The reflective learning cycle, designed by Gibbs (1988; 2013), is aimed at learning and teaching activities, but is adaptable for a range of purposes and activities.

In addition to reflecting upon digital experiences, action planning is required in order to take what you have learned from experience, information and media resources, professional conversations and networking, and from training, and to be able to apply it to the development of your digital practice. As mentioned earlier, a sample action planning tool is available on my website, but you could also develop your own. When doing this, think about the following:

- **Themes** – group together types of actions into themes. This can help reduce repetition.

- **Priorities** – you could label the themes or actions by the order of priorities. Using the asterisk symbol to label those items with top priority can be useful.

- **Timescales** – set yourself reasonable timescales and then use diary/calendar apps to make a note of when things need to be completed by.

- **To dos** – use to do list and note-taking apps to create to do lists of the individual actions, or sub-actions you need to complete. Many allow you to set reminders and alerts.

- **Links to other development** – you cannot develop digital literacy in isolation of the other CPD you undertake, so make sure that both link together.

Example

Shiraz's job as a lecturer and assessor means that he is rarely at his desk at the skills provider he works for. For most of the week he is out visiting apprentices and students in the workplace. As a result he finds it difficult to reflect on his practice, keep logs of his teaching hours and record CPD using paper forms. Instead Shiraz uses a tablet PC and his smartphone to record notes, in text, audio and image using the Evernote app and Google Keep. He has started to store templates of key documents, such as forms he needs to use with apprentices and a reflection framework to analyse his practice, and he also has an ongoing spreadsheet document on to which he records his CPD and action plans his future needs. These documents are backed up into both a Dropbox and a Microsoft Onedrive account and he uses Google Docs to edit them. These apps all connect together and make the process of editing, saving and backing up documents easy to do on his mobile devices.

Monitoring future trends

As the digital landscape is prone to frequent and disruptive change, it is important to keep abreast of new technologies and possible applications for them. This could be everything from changes in the way people are starting to carry out certain activities and functions assisted by technological solutions in their personal lives, changes to an industry practice brought about by technological advancements, or new ideas and methods in the education world which are utilising digital technologies. In this way technological advancement is changing society. In order to think about the different types of interactions, activities and functions which could change, see Chapter 3. In addition to technological advancement and innovation changing society, the opposite may also happen, with alterations required by bodies and institutions using technologies to change practice at an organisational and delivery level. This could be government education policy changes, curriculum changes and changes to funding structures. While these changes can be difficult, they can also be catalysts for creativity and innovation with digital technologies, allowing us to look at practices and use technologies to find new ways. Sometimes, both types of change are happening at the same time, and knowledge of both trends in emerging technologies and in policy in the FE and Skills sector can be useful for shaping your practice and CPD.

The process of monitoring today's trends and using them to make informed predictions about the future, or futurology as it is known, is a growing and important concept in education. This is, in part, due to rapid technological changes which continue to shape society, and with it, society's needs of education.

One organisation which is well respected in making future trend predictions about how technological and societal changes might affect education is the New Media Consortium (NMC). This US-based organisation is an international consortium of universities, researchers, colleges and other bodies interested in educational and technological research, which has established itself as the leading body of educational future trends. Its *Horizon Reports* (NMC, 2015), which have been published annually since 2004, are hotly anticipated publications which have made reliable predictions over the years, including the growth in mobile device ownership and the needs to embrace these in devices in classroom teaching, as well as the personalisation of technology, and with it the personalisation of learning. It is therefore, worth reading the latest edition of the report and picking out areas which could relate to your practice, and more widely across the FE and Skills sector. This can then be recorded in your action plan.

In addition to this report, it is also worth monitoring the websites and social media feeds of relevant professional bodies, government agencies, curriculum bodies and subject specialism bodies.

Activity

To manage the process of monitoring these bodies for changes, try setting up a dedicated feed/list of bodies and agencies to monitor. You could do this by:

- *Signing up to email mailing lists on agency and body websites – you could control this by choosing to receive a digest of the emails either weekly or monthly, and configuring your email account so that emails from these bodies and agencies are filtered directly into one email folder.*

- *Receiving social network/media updates – both LinkedIn and Google+ have features allowing you to control updates from the organisations and groups you follow. Therefore, by following these agencies and bodies, or interested professional discussion groups you can receive updates and control them in a similar way to email above. If you are on Twitter, you may*

(Continued)

(Continued)

> want to add the Twitter accounts of agencies and bodies into one list, so that you can monitor it for updates when you have time. The main disadvantage of this could be the instantaneous nature of Twitter, which could lead to some key resources and important conversations being missed.
>
> - **Receiving RSS (Really Simple Syndication) feeds** – RSS feeds allow you to monitor particular websites for new content, such as news and blog items. In recent years the availability of RSS feed aggregators, which allow you to follow and receive RSS feeds has decreased. Search for current RSS aggregators/readers on a search engine to find those still available.

Summary

In this chapter you have learned:

- About undertaking skills development and the metacognitive process.

- About reflecting upon your digital literacy development and methods for doing so.

- How to action plan for the next step in your digital literacy development.

- How to monitor and use future trends.

References and further reading

Flavell, J H (1979) 'Metacognition and cognitive monitoring: a new area of cognitive-developmental inquiry', *American Psychologist*, 34 (10): 906–11.

Gibbs, G (1988; 2013) *Learning by Doing: A Guide to Teaching and Learning Methods*. Online ed. Oxford: Oxford Brookes University. Available at: http://shop.brookes.ac.uk/browse/extra_info.asp?prodid=935.

Hartman, H J (1998) 'Metacognition in teaching and learning: an introduction', *Instructional Science*, 26 (1–2): 1–3.

Jisc (2014) *Developing Digital Literacies*. Available at: http://www.jisc.ac.uk/guides/developing-digital-literacies.

NMC (2015) *Horizon Reports*. Available at: http://www.nmc.org/publication-type/horizon-report/.

Schraw, G (1998) 'Promoting general metacognitive awareness', *Instructional Science*, 26 (1–2): 113–25.

Society for Education and Training (2015) *REfLECT+*. Available at: https://set.et-foundation.co.uk/professionalism/reflectplus/.

White, J P (2015) *CPD Resources*. Available at: http://teachdigitalliteracy.com/resources/cpd/.

The Digitally Literate FE and Skills Teacher Framework mapped against the sector professional standards

This table shows the framework mapped against the sector professional standards. The links to the professional standards in the right-hand column should be used as a guide to show how developing your digital literacy can improve your professional practice. Read through each of the professional standards on the Society for Education and Training's website (SET: 2015) to see the full details of each standard, and to frame your development around them.

The seven strands of digital literacy	Description	The professional standards this strand links to (see the SET (2015) website for a full description of each standard)
1. Understands their own position as a digitally literate professional and the relationship between skills and practice.	Understands what digital practice means for professional teachers in the FE and Skills sector. Identifies the knowledge and skills required and is able to shape their own development around them.	Professional values and attributes: 2 Professional knowledge and understanding: 7, 9, 10 and 12 Professional skills: 15, 19, 20
1.1 Understands their own digital needs, abilities and practice, and plans for their own development.	Understands their own digital needs in relation to skills, practices, knowledge and understanding and capabilities, while adopting a set of digital principles. Looks at their current practice, as well as that of others and uses this to plan for their own development. Understands the debate around digital abilities and capabilities and recognises that everyone should be encouraged to develop functional IT skills and digitally literacy.	
1.2 Understands the relationship between digital literacy and their subject area(s).	Understands the digital needs and demands of their own curriculum and subject area, as well as those of funding and regulatory bodies. Is able to use their digital literacy to embed appropriate digital learning.	
2. Recognises learners' digital needs, abilities and practice, and plans learning around the development of relevant digital skills.	Understands the issues around learning in the digital age, digital exclusion/inclusion and equality of access. Understands learners' digital needs, abilities/skills, practices, knowledge and understanding. Considers this against other factors such as background, aspirations, and general abilities. Takes this knowledge and uses it to inform teaching, learning and assessment.	Professional values and attributes: 1, 2, 3, 4, 5 and 6 Professional knowledge and understanding: 8, 11 and 12 Professional skills: 13, 14, 15

The seven strands of digital literacy	Description	The professional standards this strand links to (see the SET (2015) website for a full description of each standard)
3. Selects appropriate digital tools and seeks to use them creatively, critically and productively.	Identifies and understands the range of software (apps, digital tools, social media and services) and hardware (classroom technologies, mobile devices and specialist equipment) available.	Professional values and attributes: 1, 3 and 4 Professional knowledge and understanding: 8, 9 and 12 Professional skills: 15 and 20
3.1 Understands and uses digital technologies in professional practice creatively and critically.	Is willing and able to use digital technologies in professional practice, experimenting where appropriate, but recognising and observing best practices, legal, policy, safety and security concerns.	
3.2 Teaches creatively with digital technologies and takes into account pedagogical concerns.	Embeds use of digital technologies into learning appropriately and encourages learner creativity through interactive and engaging activities. Understands the pedagogical theory around digital learning.	
4. Develops a critical approach to digital information and media while becoming more information literate.	Understands the principles of information literacy and applies them to their professional practice and development, as well as learning and teaching. Can distinguish between different types of digital information and media and is able to search for, find, assess, use and apply digital information. Actively seeks out and discovers digital information in order to improve teaching practice.	Professional values and attributes: 1, 2, 3 and 4 Professional knowledge and understanding: 7 and 8 Professional skills: 15, 18 and 19

(Continued)

The seven strands of digital literacy	Description	The professional standards this strand links to (see the SET (2015) website for a full description of each standard)
5. Forms and manages a professional digital identity and uses it to engage professionally.		Professional values and attributes: 2, 4 and 6 Professional knowledge and understanding: 7, 8 and 12 Professional skills: 15, 17, 19 and 20
5.1 Forms and manages a professional digital identity.	Through the use of social networks and media and other digital tools, forms a positive professional digital identity. Critically understands and engages with issues of digital footprint, reputation and capital.	
5.2 Contributes to, and engages in, digital communities in order to establish and maintain a digital identity.	Is an active creator/producer, sharer, curator and showcaser of digital content/resources. This includes sharing achievements (e.g. participation in projects, successes, publications and outcomes), participation in online communities of practice and sharing of digital content. Understands significance of engagement in digital communities to non-virtual world.	
6. Understands and leads on digital safety, security, ethical and legal responsibilities, and citizenship.		Professional values and attributes: 1, 2, 3, 5 and 6

The seven strands of digital literacy	Description	The professional standards this strand links to (see the SET (2015) website for a full description of each standard)
6.1 Understands digital safety and security concerns, and is aware of safeguarding responsibilities and procedures.	Understands legal responsibilities to children and vulnerable adults as a teacher and applies this to own practice (e.g. cyberbullying, grooming and inappropriate conduct online). Understands how equality and diversity, and the related professional standards, legislation and local policies apply to digital environments.	Professional knowledge and understanding: 7, 8, 10, 11 and 12 Professional skills: 14 and 15
6.2 Understands own legal, ethical and professional rights and responsibilities when using, creating and publishing digital content.	Understands the legal implications of using media and information from online sources and of publishing own content, including knowledge and application of copyright legislation, licensing and issues around plagiarism and acknowledgement of sources.	
6.3 Understands the definition of digital citizenship and recognises the rights and responsibilities we each have in digital environments.	Understands how we are digital citizens with rights and responsibilities, and is able to develop own practice around this. Understands how actions online can have real world significance.	

(Continued)

(Continued)

The seven strands of digital literacy	Description	The professional standards this strand links to (see the SET (2015) website for a full description of each standard)
7. Plans for continuous professional development (CPD) and tracks digital trends. Makes use of digital tools for reflection.	Reflects upon their own development of the other six strands and action plans for future development. Uses the insights and tools to monitor future digital trends and uses them to improve their own knowledge and skills. Is able to use appropriate digital tools to enable reflection.	Professional values and attributes: 1, 2 and 3 Professional knowledge and understanding: 7, 8, 9, 10 and 12 Professional skills: 14, 15, 19 and 20

Note:
SET (2015) *Professional Standards*. Available at: https://set.et-foundation.co.uk/professionalism/professional-standards/.

Links to digital tools, resources and systems

The following is a list of digital tools and resources mentioned throughout the book. The URLs will lead you to their main websites, giving you more information on them.

Academia.Edu – http://www.academia.edu

BBC iPlayer – http://www.bbc.co.uk/iplayer

Bing – http://www.bing.com

Blackboard – http://uki.blackboard.com/sites/international/globalmaster/

Blogger – http://www.blogger.com

Cite-U-Like – http://www.citeulike.org

Coursera – https://www.coursera.org/

Delicious – http://delicious.com

Diigo – http://www.diigo.com

Dropbox – http://www.dropbox.com

Edublogs – https://edublogs.org/

Evernote – https://evernote.com/

Facebook – http://www.facebook.com

Flickr – https://www.flickr.com

FutureLearn – https://www.futurelearn.com/

Google – http://www.google.co.uk

Google Chrome – http://www.google.com/chrome

Google Docs – https://www.google.com/docs/

Google Drive – http://www.google.co.uk/drive

Google Gmail – https://mail.google.com

Google Keep – www.google.com/keep/

Google Scholar – http://scholar.google.co.uk

Google+ – https://plus.google.com/

Gov.UK – http://www.gov.uk

If This Then That (IFTTT) – https://ifttt.com/

Instagram – https://instagram.com/

iTunes – www.apple.com/uk/itunes/

iTunes U – https://www.apple.com/uk/education/ipad/itunes-u/

JOOMLA – https://www.joomla.com/

Jorum – www.jorum.ac.uk/

Khan Academy – https://www.khanacademy.org/

Kick – http://www.kik.com/

LinkedIn – http://uk.linkedin.com

Mendeley – http://www.mendeley.com

Microsoft Internet Explorer – http://windows.microsoft.com/en-us/internet-explorer

Microsoft OneDrive – https://onedrive.live.com/

Microsoft Outlook – http://www.outlook.com

Moodle – https://moodle.org/

Moonfruit – http://www.moonfruit.com/

Mozilla Webmaker – https://webmaker.org/en-US/resources

OER Commons – https://www.oercommons.org/

PBworks – http://www.pbworks.com/

Photobucket – http://photobucket.com/

Pinterest – https://uk.pinterest.com/

Prezi – https://prezi.com/

SlideShare – http://www.slideshare.net/

Snapchat – https://www.snapchat.com/

TES Resources – https://www.tes.co.uk/teaching-resources

Trip Advisor – http://www.tripadvisor.co.uk/

Turning Point – http://www.turningtechnologies.co.uk/

Twitter – http://twitter.com

Udacity – https://www.udacity.com/

Vimeo – https://vimeo.com/

Weebly – http://www.weebly.com/

Wikimedia Commons – https://commons.wikimedia.org

Wikipedia – http://en.wikipedia.org

Wikispaces – https://www.wikispaces.com/

WIX – http://www.wix.com/

Wordpress – https://wordpress.com/

Yahoo! – http://uk.yahoo.com

YouTube – https://www.youtube.com

Zotero – http://www.zotero.org

INDEX